Stress in
Academic Life

Stress in Academic Life

The Mental Assembly Line

Shirley Fisher

The Society for Research into Higher Education
& Open University Press

Published by the SRHE and
Open University Press
Celtic Court
22 Ballmoor
Buckingham
MK18 1XW

and
1900 Frost Road, Suite 101
Bristol, PA 19007, USA

First Published 1994

A catalogue record of this book is available from the British Library

ISBN 0 335 15720 3 (pbk)   0 335 15721 1 (hbk)

Library of Congress Cataloging-in-Publication Data
Fisher, S. (Shirley)–
    Stress in academic life/
  Shirley Fisher.
        p.   cm.
    Includes bibliographical references (p.   ) and index.
    ISBN 0–335–15721–1   ISBN 0–335–15720–3 (pbk.)
    1. College teachers – Job stress.   2. College students – Mental health.
  3. Stress (Psychology).   I. Title.
  LB2333.3.F57   1993
  378.1'2'019 – dc20   93–19667
                                                                    CIP

Typeset by Type Study, Scarborough
Printed in Great Britain by St Edmundsbury Press,
Bury St Edmunds, Suffolk

To my husband Reginald Pittman who died before this book was produced. Without his support, constant interest and lively participation, this book would never have been written.

Contents

Foreword

There is a not-too-distant image of the academic leisurely passing the hours in an ancient library in some arcadian setting far from the day-to-day pressures of the busy world. It is invoked in the World War I story of the young don being presented with a white feather and the imprecation, 'Why are you not at the front defending our civilization?', to which he replied 'Madam, I am that civilization'.

Seventy years on, all has changed. Economy, effectiveness and efficiency are with us, seemingly for ever. The new academic has now to teach increasingly more from a shrinking resource base (and salary) and in the face of an explosion of knowledge and skills not seen before. The effort of having to research, administer *and* teach (a RAT) has become considerable and, to many, unacceptable. Ways out to teach less, research less or administer less are not there and most academics will be the first to say that their lives have become stressful.

The tendency of academics to live their job, to work all hours and to sacrifice their families is widely felt by those families and, for all that they might understand their plight, there is little they can do about it. Those inventions of the devil, the phone, the fax, the photocopier and now E-mail, far from being useful crutches, have become further conduits of demand. There never was so much paper, so much to know and so much to do.

The theme of stress in academic life is therefore a timely one. Professor Fisher, who has studied the effects of stress in many circumstances, has now turned her eyes on her colleagues. She is adept at identifying the questions and observations relating to stress in the workplace and elsewhere. Her wide experience and the sharpness of her wit have added to the scholarly basis of her book and to the relevance of its targets.

It is said that reflection is the source of our humanity, of our organized thoughts and therefore of civilization itself. If by dint of unrelenting pressures to achieve, we are deprived of the time, the space, and the energy to reflect, then the bottom will have dropped out of academic life. So stress is harmful and just how harmful is the subject of this interesting text.

Professor Sir Graham Hills

Preface

It has been said that this century is the age of stress and that the experience of stress is common to all people, particularly in the Western world. Yet the levels of stress in places such as Africa and India, where the basic needs of life are often in short supply, must create a category of life-threatening experience that is beyond comparison.

Against such a perspective, stress-inducing situations that occur in work environments pale into insignificance. Yet work-related stress is none the less a real problem and its victims may be subject to considerable strain and ill health. Absenteeism levels rise and the cost to institutions may be considerable. Distress is frequently accompanied by absent-mindedness and failures of attention and memory; in conditions where sensitive tasks are part of daily work, such lapses can be very costly.

Life in academic environments has long been regarded as comfortable and privileged by many people. Perhaps the origins of this attitude are to be found in the development of medical and clerical groups in medieval times who advised kings and rulers and lived lives of relative luxury at court and then later in colleges. This privileged existence enabled them to produce scientific and scholarly works without the distraction of having to fight for survival in the world outside. Even today some dons continue to lead relatively protected lives in Oxford and Cambridge colleges.

Due principally to the financial cuts imposed on the universities by what Kogan and Kogan (1983) describe as 'expenditure-led decisions', the pressure on academics has increased; issues such as productivity and quality are now being discussed and measures for assessing these variables have been set up. It has to be said that no criteria were ever established which showed academic endeavours to have been failing. In fact, the United Kingdom university system was widely believed to be one of the finest in the world. The unseen assets associated with foreign students who came to study in Britain were probably considerable. The contacts that they made with academic staff and fellow students could be reasonably expected to provide a basis for international trade and foreign contracts.

Paradoxically, had academics actually been shown to be failing by any standards of importance, then the value of the degrees and qualifications held by those in industry, commerce and in cabinet positions in Parliament would be called into question. Yet the nature of the creative process is implicitly challenged by evaluations of productivity rates which have never been seen to be important in the past. The ability to re-work existing knowledge and have new imaginative insights might arise from periods of latent thought leading to inspiration rather than by constant demand. The task of producing new ideas and approaches is likely to be very sensitive to other pressures.

In all aspects of the work environment there will be those who create, inspire and make progress and those who are less able to do this. It would not therefore be surprising to find academics, as well as doctors, civil servants or parliamentarians who seem to be passive and who do not inspire confidence. Work populations are self-selected in that individuals apply for jobs and are then selected into work environments. This double selection process may be thought of as refining the matching of personal characteristics and talents for particular tasks. Those less suited for jobs may nevertheless interview well and be selected. Therefore, as with any work group there will be those suited and highly motivated and some who are less so, but taken overall, no evidence was provided that indicated that academics were failing.

It could be argued that expenditure-led cuts were later justified by the requirement that academics were to be subject to review. The difficulty of objectively assessing the productivity and value of ventures in arts and sciences, is so great that errors are inevitable. In some subjects, such as chemistry, small papers reporting laboratory findings can give the impression of high productivity, whereas in subjects such as psychology and philosophy, papers tend to be longer and are less abundant. Cross comparisons are difficult. Some arts subjects need little funding; sometimes just enough for a library study; others such as physics and neuroscience may need considerable resources. Power is given to some academics by virtue of their needs in resources for research. Subjectivity on the part of judges faced with many dimensional criteria is inevitable. The combined effect has been to increase the pressure on a group of individuals whose main function is to create and dispense knowledge; the effects are important.

This book examines some of the implications of recent changes in the academic world that have been created by the financial stringency that was introduced by the British Government. The issue of who manages a university not only affects salary rises, but is one of the emerging problems of higher education and how it is best organized.

The book is also concerned with the intrinsic pressures of advancement of knowledge and scholarly endeavour. Creative processes are stress-sensitive and as the pressures of the job rise, the very stability required for good quality work in science and arts is in danger of being undermined. It also examines the pressures experienced by students who are expected not only to be successful in their chosen endeavours but also to survive a number of psycho-social pressures such as major transitions away from the security of home and the financial pressures produced by meeting the escalating costs of books and domestic needs on a limited budget.

The book identifies the fundamental issue of the apparent failure of talented female students to become lecturers, senior lecturers and professors, or to function in high administration. The waste of talent if students with good degrees and PhDs are not enabled to lecture in academic disciplines and to hold posts is lamentable and unfortunate for the image of modern universities.

Finally, the book addresses the issue of the demands on academic staff and what might be done to cope with the stressful problems they report. A prevailing belief is that too much is being asked. Multiple roles as teacher, administrator and creative researcher may be too much to expect in a world of decreased funding and increased student numbers. A solution developed in later chapters is to introduce self-selected division of labour, in which academics develop a balance of chosen specialties within teaching, research and administration and are employed in accordance with match to the institution's needs.

Acknowledgements

I would like to thank Pamela Smith for helping me with some of the research that is included in the book and for her lively interest throughout. I would also like to thank my secretary Anne Crowe, for her meticulous efforts with the typing of the manuscript, the checking of the figures and the indexing. I would also like to acknowledge the role played by Bill Sutherland, Director of Personnel at Strathclyde University for useful discussions and for drawing my attention to many important issues faced by academic staff.

1

What is Stress?

The problem of definition

Stress is perhaps best seen as a broad umbrella term. The phenomena that induce stress vary greatly in their characteristics, as does the response of each individual to stress. Symptoms include depression, anxiety, obsessional, angry or phobic behaviour. Basic definitions of stress assume that it is environmentally caused but more sophisticated models assume that cognitive factors are of more importance for the majority of stresses.

Stress as an intense level of everyday life

In terms of this definition the individual's response to stress is not relevant, stress is defined by the environment. McGrath (1974) defined stress in terms of tolerance; stressful environments were considered to be those that were outside the normal tolerance limits of daily function – at extreme levels, stimulation might be perceived as pain. High temperature, fatigue, sleep loss or hunger may at intense levels constitute stress.

Although a useful tool for quantifying stress levels in the immediate external environment, the model is less useful when it comes to understanding more complex situations. Events that are common to most people's lives, such as separation and loss, moving home and difficult relations with other people, are not easy to score on an intensity measure. What must be taken into account is that what seems stressful to one person may seem challenging and exciting to another.

Stress has both positive and negative qualities. Selye (1956) introduced the term 'eustress' to describe the positive stress experience; the individual may be 'worked up' but he or she perceives it positively as a form of challenge.

Stress as an imbalance between demand and capacity

One definition that makes some sense of individual perceptions of what constitutes a stressful situation is that stress is created by an imbalance between *demand* or environmental pressure and the *capacity to meet that demand*. One model (McGrath 1974) provides the possibility of greater understanding of the psychological origins of more complex life and work stresses. For example, a person who feels that adaptation to a new situation, such as a change of job or home, is within his or her capacity would be expected to feel less stressed than someone who feels unable to meet that demand. Thus a person of high capabilities might be more able to cope with a broader range of environments without feeling stressed.

Stress and the concept of 'loss of control'

An extension of the view that stress results from an imbalance between demand and capacity, is the idea that stress is perceived whenever there is low personal control or jurisdiction over the physical, psychological or social environment. These ideas are particularly relevant to an understanding of the origins and effects of stress in occupational environments and will be discussed in later chapters. The perception of low personal control can create stress as well as exacerbate existing stresses. The relationship between the demands of a particular work or domestic situation and the level of available control is complex. The dimensions of 'demand' and 'control' are not assumed to be orthogonal, since a person may use control to reduce demand.

Figure 1.1 illustrates the notion that the world is constantly changing and presenting new challenges to the individual and that part of human motivation is to respond to such challenges. Daily events create discrepancies for the individual between the way he or she would like the world to be and the way it actually is.

It could be argued that being in control means being able to resolve these discrepancies. Thus the positive feeling of a challenge to be met may be present if control is possible, but negative states of distress may occur if there is low control. Plans for daily behaviour are evolved in which discrepancies are created. Individuals act using available control to reduce discrepancies and thus achieve the anticipated goal (Fisher 1984).

These formulations are useful in facilitating understanding of the ways in which identical life events may be perceived as positive by some

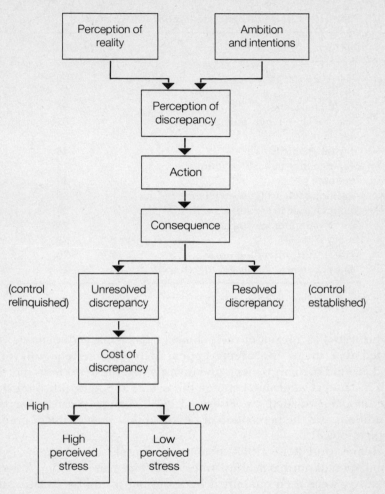

Figure 1.1   Control model of stress in life and health environments
Source: Fisher (1986).

individuals and negative by others. A situation that may appear challenging if control is possible may be distressing if it is not. Change thus creates discrepancy, the availability of personal control enables the discrepancy to be resolved.

Life change units

The role of life events such as bereavement, job loss or financial disaster in the life histories of ill people was first investigated by Holmes and

Table 1.1   Life events generated by healthy Americans

Life Change Units (LCUs)	LCU values
Death of a spouse	100
Divorce	73
Marital separation	65
Death of close family member	63
Marriage	50
Marital reconciliation	45
Major change in health of family	44
Pregnancy	40
Addition of new family member	39
Major change in arguments with wife	35
Son or daughter leaving home	29
In-law troubles	29
Wife starting or ending work	26
Major change in family get-togethers	15

Source: Holmes and Rahe (1967).

Rahe (1967) as a result of their clinical experience with patients. They noted that major life events appeared to occur frequently in the background of many patients and investigated the hypothesis that there was a causal relationship between life events and ill health. In terms of the model provided by Fisher (1984), change creates discrepant conditions and the perception of personal skill enables the discrepancy to be resolved.

Holmes and Rahe (1967) obtained a sample of life events from a population of normal healthy Americans. The events, both positive and negative, were then quantified by assigning a number relative to an arbitrary value of 50 stated to represent hypothetically the amount of adjustment created by marriage. As shown in Table 1.1 the resulting distribution of ranks showed that loss by death of a close relative was seen as the most severe and ranked first with a value of 100. The numerical values of each of the listed life stresses were used to provide an index of the amount of readjustment associated with each life event. Holmes and Rahe termed the values representing readjustment 'Life Change Units' or LCUs and predicted that the larger the values of LCUs in the recent life history of a patient, the greater the risk of illness.

Results showed that there was some predictive power. LCU scores of greater than 300 for three years predicted the risk of illness both retrospectively and prospectively. However, it has been argued that the power to predict illness is limited and particularly that the power to

Day: Wed 29th *Time:* 10 pm *Month:* April *Year:* 1987

Write a description of each problem you can remember for this day. Up to three possible problems may be recorded. Each day will probably vary. Put an 'X' in the cell against the time scale when you remember worrying about the problem. The number of times you remember worrying will vary from day to day (an example is provided so you can check that you understand the instructions).

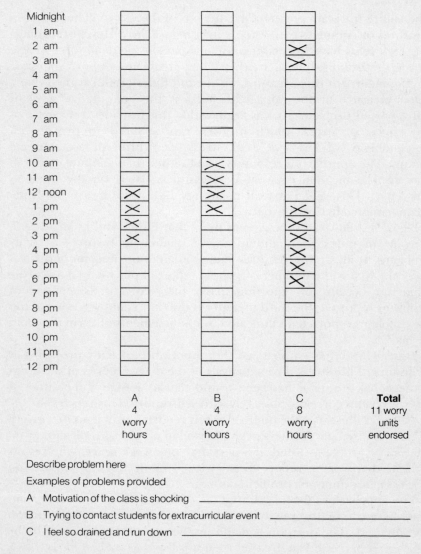

Describe problem here _____

Examples of problems provided

A Motivation of the class is shocking _____

B Trying to contact students for extracurricular event _____

C I feel so drained and run down _____

Figure 1.2 Diary used to provide data on daily problems

Source: Fisher and Elder (1992).

predict specific illness is low (Connolly 1975). Nevertheless Rahe (1989) showed some associations between cumulative life events and cardio-vascular disease, including sudden cardiac death.

Epidemiological problem analysis of life stress

The failure to obtain powerful predictions of the risk of ill health from measures of cumulative life events may reflect the different meanings that life events have for people. For one person the death of a spouse may be devastating, but for another it may create new opportunities for development. For these reasons, Fisher and Elder (1992) argued that a better measure of the impact of stress is the quantitative level of self-reported problems. It was argued that this provides a measure of the effects of stress, which in turn can be used to provide an 'epidemiology' of levels of work stress over different occupational groups. The approach is response-based rather than stimulus-based in that the classification of what is stressful is based on the person's self-report. Different personal meanings and attitudes are implicitly accommodated in this approach.

Figure 1.2 illustrates the type of diary that Fisher and Elder used to provide an index of quantitative and qualitative features of daily problems. It illustrates the three main variables or outcome measures used: the first is the number of people reported per week: 3×7 is the maximum because of reporting space; the second is the content of problems reported; the third measure is the time spent worrying about the problems reported (as indicated by endorsements of 'X' in the diary format).

Fisher (1990) has emphasized the importance of daily problems as indicators of life stress. From analysis of the diary records of different professional groups it has been found that quantitative measures of daily problems correlate positively with self-reported distress levels.

Table 1.2 illustrates the number of self reported problems of a group of male and female teachers over a period of a week as indicated by an analysis of problems listed in a personal, one-week diary. The results indicate that women report about twice as many work problems and twice as many domestic problems as men.

The approach is useful because, as outlined above, no judgement need be made by the researcher about the type of stressful situation encountered. The decision is made by the person responding. If the problem is perceived as stressful then it is listed as such. This is thus a 'person-perception' or 'response based' approach. The shift towards a response-based definition reduces the problem of interpreting personal

Table 1.2   Self-reported problems of teachers

Summary of total problem incidence and mean numbers of work and domestic problems reported per day per subject by 30 secondary school teachers in week 1 and week 2 of a four-column two-week diary study

	Week 1	Week 2	Total
% problems reported	53.1	46.9	100
Total problems	449	397	846
Work problems × per day	1.19 (0.61)	1.10 (0.79)	1.15 (0.71)
Domestic problems × per day	0.60 (0.47)	0.49 (0.39)	0.55 (0.43)

Note: Figures in parentheses represent standard deviations.
Source: Fisher and Elder (1992).

meanings because they are implicit in a person's decision that a response is stressful. This approach has proved useful in the analysis of the sources of stress in academics.

Post-traumatic stress disorder

Once described using terms such as 'shell shock', post-traumatic stress disorder (PTSD) is a response or syndrome pattern that usually occurs following very extreme levels of threat – personal attack; loss of life; inflicting injury on someone else. It is a response to very distressing circumstances that are perceived as being well outside the range of normal experience. The event concerned often gives rise to extreme terror.

The average work environment is more likely to present the minor hassles and irritations that characterize everyday life rather than such severe threats, although the stress associated with failure to achieve promotion or job loss has the capacity to create severe distress.

Some profound changes in mind function appear to be closely linked to those experiences. There is often compulsive rumination concerning the event, accompanied paradoxically by phobic avoidance of the immediate circumstances and environment surrounding the event. There is increased arousal, often panic attacks, insomnia, early waking and increased jumpiness. Aggression levels may also increase.

At least one explanation for the compulsive going over in the mind of an event now past is that it is an attempt to cope 'after the event'. Perhaps the person struggles for 'pseudo-control'. It has been suggested by Fisher (1990) in the context of the grief reaction (homesickness) associated with leaving home, that a process of replanning is occurring as old plans are incorporated into new plans for the future. Reliving features of a previous life may be a prerequisite to evolving a new set of plans and procedures. However, in the working over of old plans emotion and distress may be a by-product. In states of intense grief and distress 'obsessive review' of circumstances leading to the tragedy is often frequent.

Aspects and echoes of PTSD may occur in work environments. Those distressed, humiliated or hurt by relations with others or by perceived injustices are likely to be more absent-minded, error prone and more inward looking. At a time when universities are having conditions imposed from government, the effects in terms of competitive pressure and volume of work may be to create conditions of job stress, while at the same time reducing available control.

Summary

Stress, although widely used as a concept, is difficult to define. It may be positive or negative. The experience of stress is influenced by a number of contextual factors. The presence of high personal control has been shown to be stress reducing.

The concept of control applied to work environments provides a basis for understanding job strain and distress at work. People who are preoccupied with stressful work problems are likely to be less efficient. Stress response is multi-level and may differ in quality as well as intensity or frequently. Post-traumatic stress disorder is an extreme state usually following major events such as deaths and assaults. PTSD may occasionally feature in work environments. It is associated with vagueness, phobic states and memory loss, lapses, errors, being anxious, distracted and emotional; nightmares; panic attacks; and obsessive behaviour.

2

Stress and Efficiency in Daily Behaviour

Stress and general performance in knowledge transfer

Early work in the 1940s and 1950s on the impact of stress on aspects of performance, confirmed that stressful environments produce major changes and if sufficiently intense, have a substantial effect on attentional behaviour and performance (see Fisher 1984). Errors, lack of concentration and attentional 'drifting' or excessive focusing are frequently associated with psychological distress.

This chapter provides a rather general account of some of the main changes in attention, memory and performance in stressful conditions (further details can be obtained from Fisher 1984, 1986). The important point is that stress markedly influences many of the processes on which the acquisition, manipulation and consolidation of information depend.

Work with animals at the beginning of this century established that the greater the intensity of stimulation imposed on an animal the greater the likelihood of deterioration in its ability to remember previously learned responses (Yerkes and Dodson 1908). The Yerkes–Dodson Law, as it became known, established that for most populations an inverted 'U' curve expressed the relationship between level of arousal induced by stress and performance efficiency on a variety of different measures. The results of Yerkes and Dodson's work are presented in Figure 2.1. The graph illustrates that the probability of performance deterioration in stress varies with different tasks.

Figure 2.2 represents the Yerkes–Dodson Law in idealized form and illustrates inverted U curves for different levels of task complexity. More complex tasks have been found to be vulnerable to adverse effects of stress, whereas simple tasks may benefit from the same level of stress. These relationships were first observed with animals but have since been replicated with human beings. Later researchers have established that

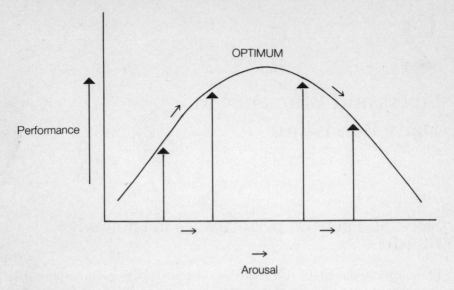

Figure 2.1   Idealized representation of Yerkes–Dodson Law
Source: Fisher (1986).

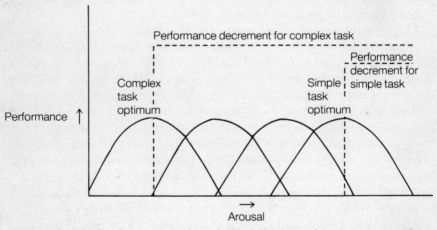

Figure 2.2   Idealized representation of task difficulty and optimum arousal
Source: Fisher (1986).

complex tasks are less vulnerable to the effects of sleep deprivation, for example (Wilkinson 1964), and more vulnerable to the effects of noise (Fisher 1983). A simple explanation of these findings is that existing levels of arousal or anxiety contribute to the general level of stress. Thus a person requires reduction of stressful stimulation to perform a complex task effectively, but may require stimulating conditions for a simple task.

These considerations are important for academic endeavour because the kinds of complex creative or problem-solving tasks undertaken by academics that require concentration, concise judgements and careful attention to detail, will be adversely affected by stress. In order to understand why this is the case, it is useful to outline some of the relevant aspects of studies of attention and memory changes in stress.

Attention and knowledge transfer

There are two identifiable aspects to attention characteristics in stress. One is *concentration* – the ability to sustain attention across a period of time. This is of critical importance in reading and creative writing, in See p13 problem solving, organizational tasks and managerial activities as well as in coping with the more mundane aspects of daily life. Individuals who have difficulty concentrating may, for example, miss critical aspects of the content of lectures or misread texts. An obvious example is where students may misread questions or fail to comprehend examination instructions.

A second identifiable aspect of attention is its *focus*. This is one of the most interesting of mind-based phenomena. Even after a great deal of experimentation, changes in attentional characteristics following stress are still little understood. From personal experience most people recognize that they have control over aspects of their own attention but they are distracted by external environmental factors or by internal states of worrying. Thus, it is possible to choose to listen to one person and not another, to watch one aspect of a complex scene and generally to choose to switch one's attention as seems appropriate. This suggests that there is attentional control. However, there are times when attention is 'captured' by the immediate environment or internal thoughts. Under those conditions, the control is lost and attention becomes fragile.

Early studies in the 1930s in Chicago (Bills 1931) established that concentration could not be sustained uniformly across time. Bills examined sequential response times to naming colours on cards and found that after a relatively short period of time, delayed response times or 'blocks' became apparent. A block was defined by Bills as a period greater than one and a half times the average response time for the task and seemed to him to involve mental fatigue creating a period when a person was no longer capable of making a response.

Some basic observations emerged from Bills' studies. First, blocking increased with time on tasks; long tasks were therefore particularly vulnerable to blocking. A rapid version of the colour naming tasks confirmed that fast response speeds were also associated with increased blocks. Equally, being tired, sleep deprived, or bored by a low stimulation task were also conditions found to be associated with blocks (see Bills 1931; Fisher 1984).

A number of environmental conditions therefore appear to be associated with response delays. Bills at first proposed a 'mental fatigue' hypothesis to account for this but found no evidence of fatigue comparable with that of physical fatigue believed to be induced by lactic acid which accumulates in muscles. Later he proposed 'mental oscillation' to account for blocks. It was assumed that a number of mental rhythms fluctuate simultaneously and that convergence of low points or 'troughs' in these rhythms are responsible for blocks.

The Cambridge theory of blocking was developed in the 1950s when Broadbent (1958) proposed 'attentional failure' as an explanation of blocking and concentration loss. In conditions characterized by boredom the attention mechanism is assumed to be more likely to switch away from one particular source to sample other sources. This would lead to an apparent response lag. Broadbent also proposed that stresses such as noise, heat and loss of sleep could cause distractions which would produce a similar effect.

Loss of concentration through boredom and distraction is important in the daily function of academic staff and students. Activities such as reading reports, listening to and delivering lectures and seminars, which are fundamental to knowledge transfer, are very stress sensitive. People are frequently required to take tests, or perform well in an interview or in public speaking tasks under conditions in which the pressures to succeed are likely to lead to a loss of concentration in some of the ways defined above.

Whilst much store is set by the spoken lecture and personally conducted tutorial sessions, accumulation of attention lapses may mean that these modes of knowledge transfer should be re-thought or where feasible replaced by self-paced and self-generated forms of learning. Obtaining knowledge by a listening–writing process with no in-built checks is vulnerable and prone to lapse. Work by Fisher (to be reported) established that there were on average between 8 and 50 self-reported periods of blocking in a one-hour lecture. This underlines the vulnerability of live lecture performance, even when lecturers are good at sustaining the attention of the class.

Ignores periodic nature

Control and distraction

The number of sources to which attention might be diverted is large. Information is being processed by all sensory systems simultaneously. A person may be aware of sounds, sights, and smells as well as of the movement of limbs, head and body. Imposed on this are stimuli from the internal environment, such as fatigue, hunger or pain signals. These signals may compete with the requirements for information processing implicit in the process of transfer of knowledge, in the live lecture. There is good reason to suppose that the lecturer also has attentional problems to cope with, students arriving late, difficult lecturing facilities etc. may distract.

On the assumption that academic endeavour is largely about the creation, transfer and manipulation of knowledge, the role of attention processes are of paramount importance in determining the nature and structure of the input. What is never noticed obviously cannot be remembered. Yet the attention processes on which knowledge acquisition ultimately depends may be very unstable. Two aspects of attention can be identified; the first is *concentration* or the ability to sustain attention on one source, the other is the *focus* of attention or selection across the range of possible stimuli.

Early work on attention involved ingenious experimenting using binary listening facilities provided by tape recorders. In one study, individuals were asked to recall information in the form of pairs of digits delivered simultaneously via headphones to each ear. The results showed that they recalled the information not in the time order in which the digits were delivered, but by ear – first one ear and then the other. It seemed that the storage and retrieval of information was generally achieved through physical channels (Broadbent 1958).

Recall by channel might be taken to indicate considerable attentional control and fits well with the subjective experience of being able to listen to one source or one mode of information at the neglect of another. However, as might be expected, the issue of attentional control is more complex. The focus of attention can be switched by sudden unexpected events such as bright lights or loud noises which can cause interruption of an on-going task. This fits with what is known of daily behaviour. A quiet environment will lead to fewer distractions when problem-solving tasks, or reading, are being done.

Early work in Cambridge showed that distractions can be as short as one third of a second on an on-going serial task when occasional bursts of noise were made to occur. It appears that the nervous system is not paralysed but that attention is switched to the noise burst briefly (Fisher

1973). Such attentional capture is evidence of some loss of control in the focus of attention.

Such distractions are likely to increase in stressful conditions because attentional demands are greater. Equally, internal sources of information such as pain, or personal problems may provide sources of distraction. Life stress factors correlate negatively with daily performance (Fisher 1984, 1986).

Personal life stress may cause impairments in carrying out work-related tasks by changing motivational features, but it also may act by providing a competing source of task information which detracts from daily efficiency on tasks. Work on oesophagitis patients (Fisher and Elder 1992) has shown that they report monitoring of personal physical health symptoms. Under these conditions it would be expected that there would be a reduction in efficiency.

Arousal and attentional selectivity

Attention changes are also responsive to biological and psychological levels of arousal. Levels of arousal can cause attention to become *blinkered* or *channelled*. At first this can result in benefits when a very complex task is being performed in that the individual will be likely to concentrate on what is really salient and essential. However, fixation on less relevant or even irrelevant aspects of a task may be common if stress levels are raised (Fisher 1984).

At very high levels of arousal verging on panic levels, attention is less likely to be blinkered or limited and more likely to be characterized by random, uncontrolled properties. Attention in these states has been described in terms of a poorly controlled attentional beam moving rapidly across the environment. One explanation is that the fast mental activity that is characteristic of a state of high arousal leaves little time available for processing signals. The individual might be likened to an engine that is running fast.

These phenomena are worth elaborating on because students often experience high levels of stress and anxiety in examination conditions. The functioning of higher mental processes is likely to be influenced in the ways outlined above. Time pressure is a major characteristic of examination conditions and, with high cost attached to failure, they are unlikely to provide reasonable conditions for the assessment of any knowledge or problem solving skill. The fact that some students still manage to do well under those conditions is important but it may be the case that these students are those with low pre-existing stress levels for a variety of reasons. People with low base arousal levels for whatever reason may benefit from the effects of stress-related stimulation because arousal increase improves mental function for low levels of arousal (see Figures 2.1 and 2.2).

Stress and errors: cognitive failures

Research initiated at Oxford by Broadbent *et al.* (1981) has shown that those who are experiencing distress appear on self-report question-naires to be error prone. Levels of 'cognitive failure' as assessed by questionnaires that require participants to report back over recent life history, the number of times that they have missed signs, forgotten events or items, etc. appear remarkably sensitive to a variety of stressful conditions.

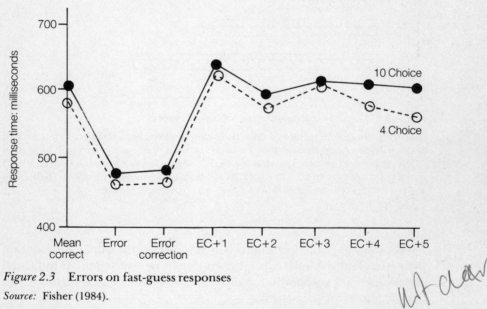

Figure 2.3 Errors on fast-guess responses
Source: Fisher (1984).

As Figure 2.3 illustrates, work on errors under laboratory conditions established that they are about one third of a second faster than correct responses (Rabbitt 1966). This implies that speeded responses are at risk for errors. Rabbitt proposed the idea that errors might be considered as 'fast guess' decisions in which the person is assumed to act before he or she has processed sufficient evidence for decision. Underlying this explanation is the notion that evidence accumulates over time in the

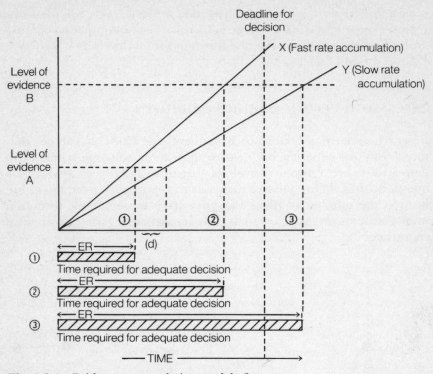

Figure 2.4   Evidence accumulation model of errors

Note: Hypothetical illustration of the relationship between characteristics of evidence and decision as joint determinants of the likelihood of error. Fast guess errors (ER) in relation to level of evidence required for decision (A, B), rate of evidence accumulation (X, Y) and deadline for decision. In no. 3 fixed deadline anticipates adequate evidence for (B) because of slower evidence accumulation (Y) – therefore errors predominate.

Source: Fisher (1984).

nervous system and that there is a finite time for adequate decision defined by features such as brightness or loudness of signal. As indicated above, speeded responding may be characteristic of high arousal and may lead to error proneness.

Figure 2.4 illustrates the hypothesis that evidence accumulates in time and that decisions made in advance of adequate evidence. Errors are '*fast guess*' decisions. However, some fast guesses may be correct by chance and others may be correct because the person already has advance information. Factors such as previous experience, knowledge of how the outside system works (e.g. the predictability of a particular set of traffic lights) will determine the proportion of fast guess responses that are errors. If a situation is perfectly predictable a person may not need the evidence for an adequate decision to be made. Under these conditions response rates could be very fast without loss of accuracy.

In summary, one global model that makes sense is the notion proposed by Fisher (1984) that *speeded processes are vulnerable*: when a person works fast, information processing time is reduced; there is an increased tendency to action rather than inaction and this will raise the probability of slips on the response generated (Broadbent 1971; Fisher 1984). As argued in the previous section, the picture of the stressed person could be likened to an engine running fast with high tendency to action.

now / really.

A final aspect that should be considered is that reduced time for care and attention because of chronic raised stress levels might create lack of organization. Papers are never filed properly; letters are lost. The background management systems that back up academic endeavour can be so neglected that the individual operates in a state of confusion. The disorganized state means increased information load and more effort to achieve a given result. Thus a negative feedback loop occurs in which stress increases.

Figure 2.5 taken from the diary of a student who was attempting to cope with a small flat with a large number of animals, illustrates the important point that life-style factors contribute markedly to stress. The errors reported could be argued to be inevitable given the pre-existing living conditions. The stressed person may be the person who creates living conditions that eventually leads to errors. Failing to find the time for organized filing and categorization can create an error prone life style as illustrated by Figure 2.5.

Summary

Stress influences cognitive activity, often quite markedly. The parameters of attention and memory are likely to change. There is an inverted U relationship between arousal and performance. At high levels of arousal there is an increased tendency for attention to become blinkered and short-term memory to be suppressed. Errors and lapses are more likely in stressful work environments and during periods of emotional distress. Overall, high academic pressure on students and staff is likely to have a negative impact on quality of performance. The trade-off between pressure to improve standards or quality control and ultimate performance is likely to be complex and pressure from this could be counter-productive.

Note from subject who took part in diary study and reported high error rates

---

I have a husband, 8 cats and 3 dogs. That is a lot of animals and people to inhabit a one-bedroomed flat. The animals all cluster on and around the bed at night and they follow us about from room to room during the day, especially if they are hungry or we are preparing food, etc. So they very definitely 'get under your feet'. I stand on them so often, not because I am clumsy, but because often there is very few bits of floor left unoccupied for me to walk on. Very often it's like an obstacle course in our house, especially at feeding time!

Sample from diary:

Wed 14th	Tripped over cat. Forgot to put chair in front of fridge to stop animals getting in and eating contents.
Thur 15th	Stood on Dillan's ear (One of the dogs). Forgot to get milk.
Fri 16th	I had just put dogs back on lead after a run. Instead of giving them a biscuit I let them all off the lead by mistake.
Mon 19th	Tripped over cat. Stood on Zippy (One of the dogs). Stood on Dillan's ear (He has very large ears). Banged knee against dressing table.
Wed 21st	Bought six items in shop, only put five in bag.
Thur 22nd	Tied dogs outside shop, went in shop and bought a few things, left shop and went up the road without dogs. Tripped over Zippy. Forgot to wind clock.
Fri 23rd	Forgot to get butter.
Sat 24th	Stood on Zippy when I got out of bed.
Mon 26th	Tripped over cat. Forgot to switch immersion heater off.
	etc . . .

Figure 2.5   Errors by student in overcrowded conditions

Source: Fisher (1984).

3

Life, Stress and Health

Psychosocial background and health

Social contexts and background conditions have long been associated with risk factors in disease and with shorter life expectancy. As indicated earlier, life stress factors such as personal loss, bereavement and divorce have been found to be associated with high morbidity and mortality risks. Historically, such findings once formed the basis of psychosomatic medicine but more recently have formed part of modern medical science. Increasing recognition is being given to the role played by psychosocial factors in mental and physical health (Fisher and Reason 1988) and the challenge for scientific endeavour is very great.

The occurrence of epidemics during social change associated with mass migrations has been established in research since the turn of the century. Of course the occurrence of epidemics can be attributed to factors such as exposure during travel, poor health conditions and housing, poverty and overcrowding, but cultural climates may operate to increase the risk of disease, because of environmental conditions, behaviour, dietary or exercise habits. The possibility of more direct connections between stress and ill health via physiological and biochemical factors, remains a possibility.

Tuberculosis has long been of interest in that, statistically, the evidence supports a strong association between the disease and conditions of war, migration, relocation, industrialization, urbanization and poverty. There are numerous citations in the research literature. Increases in tuberculosis morbidity and mortality were recorded for the Navajo and Sioux Indians who were relocated within the United States. The relocation of Irish immigrants to the USA and of Bantu natives in South Africa from the vicinity of Johannesburg into the outskirts of the city are other examples (McDougall 1949; Moorman 1950). When immigrants returned to their native villages, the infections were established there too. However, the link with stressful transition is underlined in that although up to 73 per cent of village children were affected, mortality in those cases remained low. In the case of the Irish immigrants, there is even greater support for a link with stress, because although they encountered a more affluent and potentially positive living environment, the tuberculosis incidence levels were 100 per cent greater than in those left behind in Ireland.

An important contribution is made by the research literature demonstrating that moves have important psychological effects on individuals. Unfortunately, although perhaps unavoidably, studies of relocation have confounded a number of potentially stressful circumstances, making it difficult to determine whether moving itself is a critical factor or whether circumstances created by moving are responsible for adverse psychological effects. Thus, although a positive association between moving and increased susceptibility to mental and physical ill-health has been indicated, the reason is not easily identified. For example, Faris and Dunham (1939) established that residential status in a large city (defined by home ownership as compared with rented accommodation) was related to mental health. Poor status was associated with an increased incidence of schizophrenia and depression. However, the causal direction remains unclear; areas of the city are associated with high levels of social disorganization and poverty. The possibility of self-selection by downward mobility, or 'social drift' through personal inadequacy and lack of ability to cope cannot be ruled out.

Evidence for the effects of moves on psychological state was provided by Fried (1963) in a study of enforced slum clearance. Adverse psychological effects akin to grief and depression were experienced by those forced to move to new housing. The fact that adverse psychological changes were experienced even by those moving to better housing underlines the stressful aspects of moves. Moves are in fact the third most frequently reported precipitants recalled by clinically depressed patients (Leff *et al.* 1970), which emphasizes the close relationship with mental disorder.

Although the positive relationship between mobility and physical illness has been established in the research literature, causal relationships are difficult to ascertain. However, an important longitudinal study by Stokols *et al.* (1983) showed that, in general, individuals with a high mobility history were more likely to report illness symptoms following a relocation for a new job than those reporting a low mobility history.

The relationship between psychological state and health is further confirmed by work on marital status and disease risk.

Evidence of the importance of marital status as a factor influencing

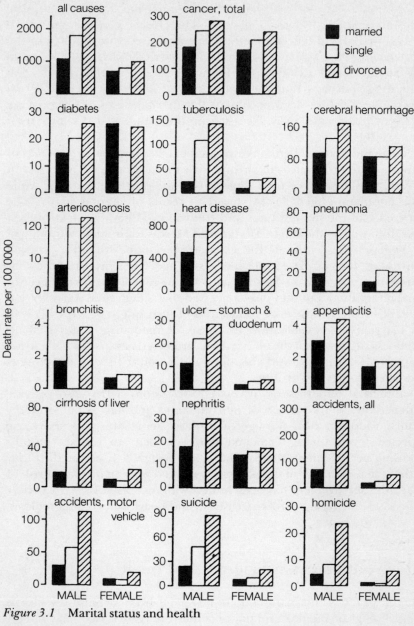

Figure 3.1 Marital status and health

Source: Fisher (1984).

health is indicated by a number of epidemiological studies. Figure 3.1 illustrates some of the epidemiological data provided by Berkson (1962), which show a statistical association between marital status and physical ill-health amongst American citizens. The effects, generally apparent for both males and females, confirm the increased susceptibility of the divorced and the single as compared with married individuals. The data also illustrates that accidents and homicide rates are similarly affected, suggesting, perhaps that the behaviour of the individual plays an important role. The fact that comparable marital status differences are apparent for suicide, provides a strong indication that the important factor is stress.

Dodge and Martin (1970) investigated marital status in the context of between-state differences in chronic disease incidence in the USA. In 1950, USA statistical records showed that the death rate for the white male population aged 35–44 varied in terms of marital status. The divorced had the highest rates and the widowed had the next highest rates, followed by the single. Dodge and Martin found that, although at all age levels the death rate for widowers was higher than for married individuals, the gap closed with increasing age. They favoured the view that marital status is a mediating factor because it represents a degree of social integration, but they also conceded that a degree of self-selection could be involved – the most robust and healthy might be more likely to get married. An explanation in terms of mediating states such as loneliness suggests that the married are protected because of the marital support offered. However, this does not account for the differences between non-married groups.

National Health records in the UK (Connolly 1975) also provide evidence on the interaction of marital status and age as vulnerability factors: widowers over the age of 55 have mortality rates above the expected levels for age-matched married men. In the six months following bereavement, the risk levels are particularly elevated. It may be that the psychological state of grief is linked with an increased risk of ill-health. Bereavement has been linked with increased risk of a variety of diseases, including coronary disease and heart failure, tuberculosis, diabetes, and cancer.

Life events, work efficiency and health

The role of life events in the aetiology of ill health is increasingly a focus of psychological, medical and popular interest. As described in Chapter 1 a series of studies by Holmes and Rahe arising from the clinical observation that life events such as job loss, divorce and bereavement seemed to feature in the protocols of patients being treated for illness, led to the construction of a scale – the Schedule of Recent Experiences.

This consisted of a spectrum of personal, social and occupational life events. A stress level weighting factor was introduced: judges were provided with a list of 42 life changes, one of which – marriage – was given a value of 500, and asked to provide life change unit values (LCUs) relative to this for the rest of the life events. Death of a spouse, divorce, marital separation, death of close family member, and detention in jail occupied the top places in terms of those events that were perceived to be the most stressful.

Early retrospective studies (for example, Holmes and Rahe 1967) showed that there had been an increase in LCUs in the two years prior to illness. The effect was non-specific and did not predict the type of illness. The studies suggested that below LCU values of 150, there was no reason to expect ill-health; between 150 and 300 LCU, approximately half the individuals reported an illness in the following year. For 300 LCU the level was 70 per cent. A later study involving 2,500 US Navy officers (Rahe and Lind 1971) identified a build-up of LCUs prior to illness. Following the illness, LCU totals remained elevated. The LCU score is assumed to represent the amount of adjustment required by change.

Figure 3.2 illustrates a conceptualization of processes by which the experience of a life event might increase the risk of infectious or chronic disease. First, the life event might give rise to adverse prevailing conditions (poverty, overcrowding, etc.) resulting in greater encounters of antigens or more encounters with new antigens. The second possibility is that the individual's behaviour changes as a response to stress and that the risk of bodily malfunction or antigen encounter changes as a result. Finally, irrespective of the nature of the life event, the mental and physical state of the individual changes as a function of stress: a person may become more biologically aroused, or more worried and preoccupied.

Models of common denominators of life stress events

Social disruption and anxiety

One factor examined by those seeking to understand the relationship between stress and ill-health is that of social disruption. There are a number of slightly different focuses, but the general argument is that the individual exists in that context and life events create changes within this context which lead to and maintain raised anxiety. Periods of rapid

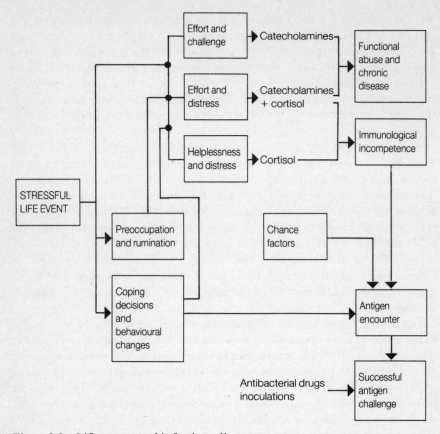

Figure 3.2   Life events and infectious diseases
Source: Fisher and Reason (1989).

change as currently typical of academic institutions might create chronic instability.

Wolff (1953) formulated some main postulates which he argued could provide a basis for understanding the increased risk of illness as a response to change. Changes affect the folklore and taboos of a culture and the threats created by these taboos often become over exaggerated and create anxiety. Formal methods for dealing with those threats are part of the culture but massive cultural change reduces the scope of familiar methods for dealing with it. Finally, Wolff argued that situations of rapid cultural change create cultural pressures but remove techniques for anxiety-reduction: 'The participant mistrusts habits and intuitions, and social experience no longer leads to a common sense of values'.

Status integration

Research by Dodge and Martin (1970) was stimulated by an interest in the rise in chronic disease levels in the USA, by within-state differences in chronic disease levels, and also by differences in sub-populations as a function of age, race and marital status.

Dodge and Martin founded a social stress theory to account for within- and between-state differences in the incidence of chronic diseases such as heart disease and neoplasms. For example, 1951 mortality rates for New York were 938.5 (per 100,000) for heart disease and 238.9 (per 100,000) for malignant disease, whereas in Mississippi rates were 488.4 and 163.3 respectively. They found that there were better correlations between chronic disease levels and suicide levels than infant mortality per state. They argued that their findings support a stress-based explanation for the increase in chronic disease rather than lack of health care resources which would have led to raised infant mortality rates.

The role status consistency model

Totman (1979) noted that social factors exert a protective influence on health. The individual is susceptible to illness when social mobility or status incongruity occurs. He proposed a structural theory that assumed that each individual is equipped with a set of prescriptive rules. For these rules to exist they must be resistant to change, although some clarification or refinement can occur as the result of social interactions. Social change creates a situation where the rules break down. Exits, losses, marital disharmony could all be seen in terms of the breakdown of rules. For example, a bereaved person, in addition to grieving for a lost loved one, may also lose an aspect of his or her identity and may have to evolve new status in the community. Oatley (1988) develops a similar approach as part of his cognitive model of social identity. Those encountering severe life events and low social support are particularly at risk, although some 'hardy' individuals seem able to exist with very low social support.

The details of how social disharmony creates increased risk of illness need to be explored in detail. One possibility is that anxiety levels increase and that there is long-term damage to health because of states of preoccupation causing distress and unhappiness. The hormone states associated with distress have been argued to create functional damage. However, there may be different psychobiological dynamics operating, which vary as a function of time following social change.

Gilbert (1988) has considered the importance of loss of social status in a psychobiological theory of depression. He proposes a model of the reaction to change and loss, in which active searching, accompanied by raised anxiety, is the first phase. A 'stop' phase in which the person suffers feelings of helplessness and gives up, follows later. Thus an initial phase of struggle in the case of irreversible loss is later followed by apathy and distress. Ultimately health damage is best explained either in terms of changes in mental function or as a consequence of prolonged high levels of activating hormones (catecholamines and cortisol).

The control model

Fisher (1986) proposed that life events create changes in the level of demand together with reduction of control over various aspects of the new life-style. Reduction of control occurs when a person feels unable to produce a set of actions that will restore the perceived discrepancy between reality and personal aims and ambitions. Change both creates discrepancies and, introduces novelty, which in turn may decrease the level of control a person experiences in relation to the environment.

There is considerable evidence to suggest that perceived control is a major factor in the response to stressful situations. A person who perceives that he or she can take effective action is less likely to experience stress than one who does not. It seems intuitively obvious that a person with control will use it to solve a problem that is causing stress. In other words daily hassles and difficulties may become stressful if there is no way of controlling them.

These issues are particularly pertinent to the understanding of the impact of work environments and especially to the lives of academics where role definition and job descriptions are ambivalent and power or status in the organization is unclear. Academic staff might fulfil a number of roles simultaneously: freelance writer; scientist; artist; teacher or journalist, all with many different daily work commitments and responsibilities, but with no effective means of influencing government policy or aspects of student commitments to students.

The nature of competitive environments is often such that social support is not forthcoming. Limited funds mean limited promotional prospects and this may influence support provided in the academic environment. The combination of erosion of control and the possibility of attenuated social support could well influence perceived stress at work for academics.

Summary

Life and work stresses have a marked effect on behaviour and health. Various models have been proposed to account for the relationship between life stress and health. One possibility is that change and disruption are common denominators of many life stress experiences such as job loss, financial difficulty, moving, all of which influence risk of ill health. A second possibility is that most major life events create a reduction of personal control over life. These are important considerations because in the case of academics, there has been a reduction in personal jurisdiction and control in academic life as a result of changing demands.

4

Stress and Control as Factors in Health and Well-being

The importance of personal control

This chapter outlines the evidence demonstrating the importance of personal control in a variety of environments. The theory developed provides a possible important basis for understanding academic stress.

Control is best defined as jurisdiction or discretion in relation to daily events and situations. Two types can be identified: the presence of control for its own sake; and the availability of control over stressful problems.

Early interest in personal control was developed by Hendrick (1943) who proposed that there was an innate tendency to control and manage the environment. He proposed that the ability to master one's environment is perceived personally as pleasurable. The desire to do so was assumed to be so fundamental that it was assumed to form part of a major developmental drive. In a variation of this, Fernichel (1945) proposed that the perception of control was not necessarily pleasurable in its own right but was anxiety reducing. White (1959) claimed that the exercise of competence is extremely important and that it provides control. He also saw it as a major positive drive. Looked at from these points of view, erosion of control by government or institutional prescription would be likely to increase stress.

Stress and control relationships

Perceived control is important with regard to threatening situations, such as may occur in work environments, because of the power it gives to attenuate or reverse unpleasant events. Thus control is really the means of damping the effects of life stresses. Millar (1979) took this further and proposed the 'minimax hypothesis'. This assumes that individuals act to minimize maximum danger.

This damage limitation view of the use of personal control provides a very useful approach. The hypothesis requires flexibility in interpretation however, because there are many situations where control is apparently lost voluntarily. For example, consulting a doctor or dentist could be argued to involve the relinquishing of control. Research has not demonstrated direct links between the loss of control and stress in these situations, but it may be an important element of the anxiety often associated with clinics and hospitals.

Fisher (1984) proposed that the pleasure derived from controlling the environment and the ameliorating effects of control on daily stress can be understood by the *discrepancy reduction* model. The individual always acts to reduce the discrepancy between reality (the way the world is) and his or her needs or requirements (the way the world should be). Successfully reducing discrepancies created by daily life can be both pleasurable in its own right and can reduce stress.

Seen in this way, life situations are like games of chess where moves and counter-moves are made to achieve an end result. This is in keeping with an approach developed by Miller, Gallanter and Pribram as early as 1960 in which human behaviour was conceived in terms of hierarchically organized plans. Behaviour was assumed to be planned with the possible consequences of the action in mind. In this sense being in control means being able to effect plans that reconcile the discrepancy between actual reality and ambition.

Animal studies of instrumentality

Work with animals exposed to electric shock has made a major contribution to the understanding of the importance of the availability of instrumental responses that facilitate avoidance of, or escape from, noxious stimulation. The research literature contains an interesting contradiction: although the weight of evidence suggests that absence of an appropriate instrumental response (helplessness) results in more stressful symptoms than conditions where control is available. Studies on primates by Brady (1958), have confirmed that having some forms of control may be extremely stressful. Monkeys who could avoid shock by pressing a lever every 20 seconds developed gastrointestinal ulcers, whereas the yoked controls did not.

Weiss (1971) argued that the experimental set-up used by Brady did not involve the provision of adequate coping feedback. Fisher (1984) developed the argument further in suggesting that in cases where a person operates 'control by avoidance', i.e. taking some form of action to avoid an encounter, then cognitively he or she will be in a state of perceived helplessness because avoidance does not provide feedback.

However, Weiss (1968) also criticized the design of these experiments on the grounds that the monkeys who were given instrumental control ('executive monkeys') had been pre-selected on the basis of their ability to learn avoidance responses on pre-experimental trials.

Although generalization from animal studies is difficult, these studies provide a hint that different designs involving instrumentality may involve different forms of control. In particular, it is useful to distinguish 'control by direct avoidance', whereby if the response is successful the animal does not receive the punishment but neither is there any appropriate feedback to show that responding is successful, from direct control where action directly cancels the problem.

Control by avoidance features in occupational contexts when a person exercises control over his own behaviour or a product to avoid another person's displeasure. Thus compliance with work procedures or deadlines in order to avoid confrontation may be a source of stress in that the person never has feedback concerning the effectiveness of the behaviour in preventing confrontation. Because of this lack of feedback, behaviour typical of loss of control may dominate and confidence be reduced. This may account for the finding that people with phobic avoidance become more avoidant and more anxious with increasing passage of time.

Human studies of self-administration of shock

Studies in laboratory settings using electric shocks on human beings have focused on self-delivery of the shock as compared with it being experimenter-delivered. The findings, if anything, indicate personal preference for and greater psychological tolerance of self-administered shock.

Early studies by Haggard (1943) showed that self-administered shock resulted in smaller skin conductance changes than experimenter-induced shock, and was perceived as less unpleasant. In addition, the response to shock was more readily extinguished and subjects were more aware of contingencies. However, self-stimulation confounds the effects of control with those due to predictability of events. The individual who can predict and therefore prepare to receive stimulation, can contemplate a strategy for reducing its effects, and can experience 'safety' in inter-signal intervals (Seligman 1971).

Pervin (1963) carried out a detailed study of the twin roles of prediction and control under conditions of threat, in order to try to partition the effects of control and predictability. Control was manipulated by either allowing the subject to control the application of electric shocks (S-control), or allowing the experimenter to have control (E-control). There were three conditions of predictability (signal; no signal; inconsistent signal) provided by means of three different lights that indicated when the shock would occur. The subject had one switch that produced shock and another that did not, but which allowed shock to be E-controlled. The data collected included: preferences – the subject was asked to indicate which of the conditions was preferred; pain ratings; anxiety ratings; subjective reports of experiences; and reaction times for decisions.

Results showed that in terms of personal assessment there was preference for personal control. A number of reasons were provided: subjects imagined that shock duration might be shortened; greater correspondence between switch and shock was believed to reduce surprise; mastery, freedom and choice were seen as desirable. Those subjects who disliked personal control reported that it resulted in conflict about whether to press the switch or not; it increased concentration on anxiety-producing signals; it represented unnecessary punishment of the self.

Studies on self-administered shock are important in that there is some indication of individual differences in the preference for self-administration. In a study by Ball and Vogler (1971), subjects were given an initial choice of being self-shocked or machine shocked. Preference was assessed in terms of whether subjects developed a consistent pattern of self-shocking or machine-shocking. After seven randomly delivered shocks (machine shock), a subject was given experience of self-delivered shocks and was then given the choice of continuing with self-delivery but at a cost of receiving two shocks in quick succession rather than one.

Of 39 subjects, 25 chose self-shock in preference to machine shock and 21 of these subjects claimed that it was to avoid uncertainty. Those 25 subjects were then given a choice between single machine-shock and double shock which was self-delivered. As might be expected, because of the penalty of experiencing twice the frequency of shock, only about a third of subjects continued with their original self-shock choice. The study contributes useful information about possible reasons for accepting machine-shock conditions. Out of the 11 subjects who chose machine shock originally, 4 subects were prepared to accept the double-shock penalty rather than change. One of the most important results of these studies is to emphasize that there may be different 'targets' or aims by which level of control is judged. In the study by Ball and Vogler (1971), one of the subjects who had opted for double machine-shock responded 'I am very resistant to authority. I thought that you wanted to see if I could take self-shock when the machine began to give me two shocks.' A second subject reported choosing double machine-shock because 'I thought that by taking double shocks the experiment would end in half the time.' Yet another subject evolved a different logic for machine-shock: 'The possibility of not getting shocked exists if you do not do it to yourself.'

The authors of the study refer to these reported strategies as 'deviant', and emphasize that investigation of the reasoning involved shows sources of reinforcement involving idiosyncratic and distorted views of the experiment. This raises the issue that the perception of control is not only situationally influenced but may also depend on personal meanings that are attached to particular situations. Individuals may perceive a situation in terms that will enable them to accept the worst, find an interpretation that makes the worst palatable, or may seek out the worst in order to gain long-term advantages. In even simple threatening situations where there appears to be a loss of control, passivity and helplessness may be a yet more subtle form of the exercise of control.

In an autobiography by Dolgun (1965) of his experiences as a victim of interrogation procedures in the Soviet Union during Stalin's regime, a similar theme is echoed in that Dolgun implies that he gains esteem and satisfaction from controlling the behaviour of the guards by determining whether or not they punished him, fooling them. Fisher (1984) termed this 'control by irrelevant means' since there was no control over (relevant) sources of deprivation and punishment.

Stress in work environments

Figure 4.1 illustrates the approach developed by Karasek (1979), based on studies of 2000 Swedish and American workers. Two dimensions are recognized, the level of control or personal discretion and the level of threat or demands made on a person.

Karasek's model would identify low-rank and low-grade jobs as those most likely to be in the high-demand, low-control quadrant and therefore to be associated with job distress. By contrast the executive job with high personal jurisdiction is likely to be associated with job challenge.

As Figure 4.1 illustrates, when both the levels of demand and control are high the outcome is perceived as challenging and positive. However, when the level of demand is high but control is low the outcome is

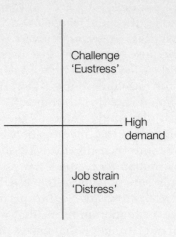

High control (discretion)

Challenge
'Eustress'

High
demand

Job strain
'Distress'

Low control

Figure 4.1   Karasek's Job Strain Model (simplified representation)
Source: Adapted from Karasek (1979).

perceived as negative; a state of distress. Thus positive and negative forms
of work stress may be determined by the degree of executive control a
person has over aspects of the job. This formulation may be simplistic in
that 'demand' and 'control' are unlikely to be orthogonal but represent
interactive dimensions. People use avoidable control to reduce demand
levels. Thus, distress at work may depend on complex factors including
the perceived availability of the means for control and the perceived skill
and capacity required to make use of facilities.

The potential importance of this model is illustrated by Figure 4.2
which shows the results of a study in the car industry where poor mental
health was associated with low grades of employment. Those who were
low skilled shop-floor workers were most likely to have poor mental
health and greater risk of cardiovascular disease.

The indication that subjects do not have to operate the instrumental
means of control in order for instrumentality to be effective is provided
by Glass and Singer (1972). Their studies showed that, at least for
human subjects, the mere belief that the means exist for exercising control over noxious stimulation is sufficient to reduce its unpleasant effects
on behaviour and to increase tolerance of the situation. This means that
the assumptions people make about their immediate work and home environments will have an important impact on perceived threats.

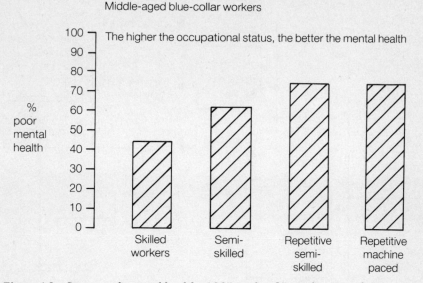

Figure 4.2   Status and mental health: 1965 study of Detroit car workers
Source: Internal report.

Stress and health outcome

The above issues are of importance in drawing attention to the role of stress in increasing disease risks for individuals. What is largely unknown is the underlying mechanism, but the physiological response to stress may play a part. It was originally assumed that the response to stress was uniform and bland, mediated by hormones such as adrenalin and noradrenalin (collectively known as the catecholamines), and by cortisol. In 1956 Selye wrote about what he called the General Adaptation Syndrome – a uniform state of malaise that reflected stress effects irrespective of the type of stress involved. Selye reached these conclusions by noting the symptoms of physically ill patients, attributing the malaise to the effects of stress involving the hormone cortisol.

Recent research has identified the possibility of more complex patterns in the biological response to stress. Anger is more likely to be accompanied by raised levels of noradrenalin and fear by adrenalin. Daily effort is reflected in levels of both hormones and in fact catecholamine levels increase during the day.

What is particularly interesting, however, is that cortisol is more likely to be secreted when the animal or person is in distress, whereas the catecholamines appear to reflect demand or effort (Fisher 1989).

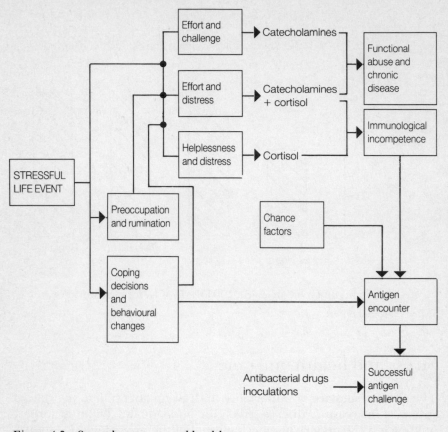

Figure 4.3   Stress hormones and health
Source: Fisher (1989).

Figure 4.3 from Fisher (1989) illustrates the possibility that raised levels of catecholamines occur when there is control available. The situation is then one of effort that is reflected in raised anxiety and tension. The long-term cost could be functional abuse of organs or physiological systems leading to anatomical damage. For example, stress hormones are associated with increased fats and fatty acids in circulation and which are likely to be deposited in the cardiovascular system especially if male hormones are present. Equally, as a rebound effect in relation to stress, acid secretion may increase in the intestinal tracts, perhaps increasing the risk of duodenal ulcer (Fisher 1990). Thus the risk of certain types of chronic disease may increase. The term 'somatization' has been introduced to describe the way in which functional abuse of bodily systems eventually comes to create anatomical change.

Recent research has also indicated, however, that the immune response to antigens may be suppressed by the presence of hormones secreted in times of distress. Prompted by the secretion of adreno-carticotrop (ACTH), the stress hormone cortisol is secreted. ACTH can itself when injected into animals suppress the immune response. Equally, cortisol appears capable of a similar effect. There is some evidence that natural killer cells can be suppressed by ACTH and cortisol (Fisher 1989; Cox 1989), so there are important implications for cancerous disease in which natural killer cells are believed to play a role in surveillance and destruction of malignant cells.

Figure 4.3 also illustrates the possibility that when control is available, effort and challenge are the likely responses to stress and the dominant hormones are likely to be the catecholamines. When control is not available, the individual may still raise his or her effort levels to struggle for control, but cortisol levels may also rise. Under these conditions there may be a risk of immuno-suppression as well as functional abuse of bodily systems. Thus the animal or person struggling in distress may be at risk from a broader spectrum of illness. The kind of illness that results may reflect chance environmental factors.

Summary

Stress occurs when personal control is low. Research on perceived control as a factor in stress has shown that there are many complex factors involved. Personality, style and personal goals may vary. What appears to be low control may mask the fact that a different form of control is being exercised. People in work environments may have different work targets that determine how personal control is perceived.

Control over all aspects of the psychosocial environment is likely to be linked to health. Reduced control may mean greater experience of chronic levels of stress but may also be associated with damaging levels of hormone in circulation which influence immunosuppression and can enhance structural deterioration in bodily systems. It is important to create work environments which are conducive to effective efforts.

5

Stress in Students

The stress of the transition to university

Moves from home to university

Change and transition are common features of life, often associated with upward mobility, but the process of change may have powerful negative effects on well being and health. Since the number of places available for applicants to university are limited, the chance to go to university is a privilege. However, even so, many students suffer in terms of mental and physical health, following the transition.

Until recently, very little was known about the experience of students making the transition from school or home to university. For most first-year students, this also involves leaving home to take up residence in a different location. The stresses that this creates for the student have been investigated relatively recently (Fisher and Hood 1987, 1988; Fisher 1989) and there is a background of research on the effects of moving home that is relevant.

In historical perspective, there are a large number of research publications concerned with the association between residential transition and mental or physical ill health. For example, for immigrant and migrant groups there is evidence of higher hospital rates for mental disorder and for chronic and infectious disease (see for example Holmes 1956; Medalie and Kahn 1973).

Such studies do not easily establish the direction of a causal link. Perhaps those who are stressed, disturbed or physically ill seek to move to a better place, or poor environmental conditions both lead to ill health and predispose a person to move. Self-selection into migration cannot be discounted.

Homesickness is a syndrome of considerable importance for the understanding of stress. The term refers to a complex cognitive

Table 5.1   The transition to university

Cognitive failure, mental health, and adjustment profiles before and after the transition in homesick and non-homesick residents[a]

	Not Homesick (n = 42)		Homesick (n = 22)	
	$\bar{\chi}$	SD	$\bar{\chi}$	SD
At home				
MHQ1	22.81	(8.6)	29.25[a]	(12.5)
Obsessional (personality)	2.61	(2.2)	3.72[b]	(2.7)
Somatic	3.21	(2.5)	4.54[b]	(2.7)
Depression	1.89	(1.6)	3.82[c]	(2.8)
CFQ1	32.64	(10.66)	36.9NS	(12.3)
Sixth week at university				
MHQ2	23.0	(11.54)	33.04[c]	(14.1)
Anxiety	3.78	(3.1)	6.48[c]	(3.7)
Somatic	2.63	(2.1)	5.17[d]	(2.9)
Depression	2.56	(2.3)	4.48[d]	(3.2)
Obsessional (symptoms)	2.54	(1.6)	3.35[b]	(2.1)
CFQ2	38.21	(11.88)	42.78NS	(13.5)
CAQ	100.69	(17.7)	84.31[d]	(18.2)
DRI	4.0	(3.2)	8.50[d]	(4.2)

Notes: [a] As designed by 'not homesick' versus three other categories of 'homesick' on self-rating scale (from Fisher and Hood 1987).
   [b] $p < 0.05$.
   [c] $p < 0.01$.
   [d] $p < 0.001$.

Sources: CFQ = Cognitive Failure Questionnaire (Broadbent *et al.* 1981); CAQ = College Adaptation Questionnaire (Cronberg 1968); DRT = Dundee Relocation Inventory (Fisher 1990).

motivational-emotional state concerned with grieving for and missing home. The importance of the experience was recognized as early as the seventeenth century in classic medical texts (Harder 1678). It seems strange that only recently has the topic been given much attention.

A recent series of studies conducted with boarding school pupils, student nurses and university students, has shown that about 60 to 70 per cent of students and school pupils report the experience of homesickness during their first term at university. For some students the experience is mild and self limiting, for others it is a profound state of grief anxiety and depression.

Table 5.1 illustrates findings for a longitudinal study by Fisher and Frazer (forthcoming) show the rise in levels of psychological disturbance following the transition from home to university. This is indexed by the Middlesex Hospital Questionnaire (Crown and Crisp 1966), which assesses disturbance in psychological state in non-clinical populations. The results show that there is considerable disturbance in the nursing population following the transition to residence in nursing college. The main features of psychological disturbance were increased anxiety, depression and obsessionality.

The figure also shows that perceived absent-mindedness increased from home to residence in college. This is a barometer of the effects of stress in these students. There are of course considerable implications for the application of nursing skills; increased absent-mindedness and actual errors can be very bad for patient care.

Theories of the effects of loss and separation

The previous chapter provides an account of four major theories which might account for the impact of change. Separation and loss are likely to produce high anxiety and distress in students leaving home for university.

Separation anxiety

Research involving separation of a young infant from its mother (Bowlby 1973), showed that separation results in anxious searching behaviour in the infant, frequently accompanied by anger and distress. After prolonged separation, the infant may become depressed and apathetic.

An obvious issue is the extent to which phenomena observed in young infants can be generalized to the state of adults. Weiss (1982) has argued that similar attachment behaviour may be present in adults. Friendships and relationships between parents and adolescent offspring or between marital partners may have many of the characteristics that Bowlby observed for young infants and their mothers; separation may therefore be a powerful factor in the lives of adults. A complete explanation of the stress that comes from separation must take account of the role individuals play in the lives of others. Even temporary loss of support can result in panic, distress and feelings of incompetence. There is as yet no complete theory of the role of other people as determinants of social cohesion or perceived isolation and loss of control.

Interruption of plans

Research on the effects of interruption on memory and task performance also provides a basis for understanding the changes in cognitive
state and mood that are part of the homesickness response. Research on
interruption is largely laboratory based; it is assumed that interruption
causes the thwarting of ongoing planned activity. This raises tension
because planned sequences of behaviour are assumed to have internal
energy. Interruption thwarts the process and the energy is released as
arousal or anxiety (Mandler and Watson 1966; Mandler 1975). There
may be enhanced memory for interrupted tasks and this effect will in
turn enhance the influence of separation.

Loss of control

It has been argued by Fisher (1984, 1986), that change and transition are
stressful because a person experiences, if only transiently, loss of control
over the new environment. The new environment will have new
properties in most cases and the individual needs to adapt to new places,
faces and routines. In some cases, as with culture shock, the individual
may be required to adapt to a new cultural climate that includes new
language, behaviour and social customs. The impact of this can
sometimes be startling (Fisher and Cooper 1991).

Psychological disturbance following transition
to university

Studies conducted amongst the Scottish universities confirmed that the
transition to university is stressful. All student groups studied, including
those who were non-resident as well as those who were newly resident,
shared increased levels of depression, obsessional symptoms and absent
mindedness within six weeks of the first term at university. These results
came from a longitudinal study in which students were contacted three
months before they left home and then again six weeks into the new
term (Fisher and Hood 1987). They were assessed with a standard
diagnostic test, the Middlesex Hospital Questionnaire. The results
indicated that psychological disturbance was raised by the sixth week of
the experience of university.

Students were additionally asked to report problems and the amount
of time spent worrying about them that occurred during this period.
Table 5.2 shows that the source of problems associated with university

Table 5.2 Problems reported by first-year students

	Home-based		Residents	
	Reports (%)	$\bar{X}WL^a$	Reports (%)	$\bar{X}WL^a$
1. *Main problem categories*				
Academic	65	2.13	61	1.89
University routines	35	1.88	24	1.53
Financial	18	1.67	47	1.66
Social	24	2.21	45	1.73
Future career at university	9	2.67	9	2.10
Family	3	2.0	17	2.63
Missing people	6	2.0	14	1.80
Health	9	2.0	14	2.0
2. *Problems specific to life-style*				
Social life	–	–	9	1.41
Domestic routines	–	–	3	1.0
Institutional (privacy)	–	–	17	0.90
Restrictions on freedom	29	1.17	–	–

Notes: [a] WL: worry level, 1 = mildly worried; 2 = very worried; 3 = extremely worried.

were categorized as 'academic', 'university routines', 'financial restraints and management'. About nine per cent of all students indicated that they had reconsidered staying on at university because of the stress.

Table 5.2 also shows that some problems were specific to resident students: aspects of social life, domestic routines and institutional features (such as lack of privacy) dominated. By comparison, home based students faced restrictions on freedom and reported problems trying to combine the demands of home life with the new demands of university.

Worry levels, defined as the number of times a student reported worrying, are greater for problems in academic, social, family and health categories. Residents were largely concerned with family and health issues.

Homesickness, as self-reported by resident students, was found to be highly frequent in the first term but diminished as the academic year progressed. For some students, however, the effect of homesickness remained throughout academic life.

Table 5.3 shows the main self-reported aspects of the concept of homesickness as reported by homesick and non-homesick resident students. It is clear that missing the home environment and home area is given as high a priority as missing friends and people. The table also

Table 5.3   Personal definitions of homesickness in first-year students

Feature categories from definitions provided	Frequency of reported features and percentage of subjects reporting each feature	
	Homesick (n = 60) f(%)	Non-homesick (n = 60) f(%)
'Missing home environment'; 'Missing house, home, area etc.'	18 (30.0)	16 (40.0)
'Missing parents/family'; 'Longing for people at home'	20 (33.3)	12 (30.0)
'Wanting to go home'; 'Feeling a need to return home'	14 (23.3)	11 (27.5)
'Missing friends'; 'Longing for friends'	18 (30.0)	5 (12.5)
'Feeling of loneliness'	3 (5.0)	7 (17.5)
'Feeling depressed'	3 (5.0)	3 (7.5)
'Missing someone close to talk to'	4 (6.7)	1 (2.5)
'Feeling insecure'	3 (5.0)	2 (5.0)
'Obsession with thoughts of home'; 'Thoughts about home'	3 (5.0)	3 (7.5)
'Feeling unhappy'	1 (1.7)	3 (7.5)
'Feeling unloved'	2 (3.3)	1 (2.5)
'Disorientation'; 'Feeling lost in new environment'	2 (3.3)	1 (2.5)
'A longing for familiar company and places'	1 (1.7)	1 (2.5)
'Thinking of the past'	1 (1.7)	2 (5.0)
'Feeling of not belonging'	1 (1.7)	1 (2.5)
'Regret that life had changed'; 'A feeling of regret'	3 (5.0)	0 (0.0)
'Feeling isolated'; 'Cut off from the world'	2 (3.3)	1 (2.5)
'Feeling uneasy'	0 (0.0)	2 (5.0)
'Feeling ill'	1 (1.7)	0 (0.0)
'Dissatisfaction with present situation'	1 (1.7)	0 (0.0)
'Unable to cope'	1 (1.7)	0 (0.0)
'Unable to do anything'	1 (1.7)	0 (0.0)
'Hating the present place'	0 (0.0)	1 (2.5)

Note: The following features were endorsed by only one person in the following groups.
   Homesick: 'Thinking that home was better than here'; 'Feeling of making a mistake';
   'Sinking feeling in stomach'; 'Loss of appetite'; 'Feeling of desperation' and 'Crying'.
   Non-homesick: 'New self-reliance'; 'Feeling of desolation' and 'Feeling unsettled'.

Source: Fisher, Murray, and Frazer (1985), and Fisher (1989).

shows the idiosyncratic nature of the experience because there are many symptoms not reported by everyone.

There were no differences in homesickness reporting between those who were homesick and those who were not. Thus there was no evidence to suggest they were using the term differently. This was an important pre-requisite for the study.

These studies, conducted across about three years, showed that males and females did not differ in their inclination to report homesickness and that within the age range studied there was no effect of age. A study in a school in the Australian outback (Fisher *et al.* 1991), was the only study that established a gender difference, finding that females were more likely to report homesickness. However, this school has a very tough physical regime and is concerned with outward bound activities and it is possible that girls find it uncongenial. There was some evidence for this and the relation of homesickness to hostile environments if positive would support the central model.

A number of vulnerability factors were identified. The distance of the move seems to be important; those who move long distances to take up residence at university seem to be more affected. There is also a control effect in the sense that those students active in the decision to come to university are more likely to react positively to the move. This may be the result of a complex self-selection factor. Perhaps those who have control over their destiny and are not forced into making a decision by parents do not got to university if they do not like the idea of it or fear homesickness.

Homesickness is in general an unpleasant and stressful experience for students. It can debilitate a student, making it difficult for him or her to study or cope effectively with academic life. As indicated earlier, for some students (about 70 per cent) the experience is mild and self limiting with greatest effects in the morning or evening. In other words, the day's activities keep it at bay. For other students, the effect is profound and enduring and is likely to have a major effect. Some of these students stayed in their rooms, missed lectures and were unable to function effectively. They were also unlikely to report the experience, even when it was causing profound depression because they believed it to be 'wimpish'. A study confirming a judgmental bias against intellectual factors in students self-reporting homesickness, by neutral judges, is reported in Fisher (1990).

Personal vulnerability factors

Students who are passive and mildly depressed prior to leaving home have been found to be those most likely to show raised levels of homesickness following the move to university (Fisher and Hood, 1987). At least one explanation is that this was because of an inability to become committed to the new environment and to make use of distracting, pleasant conditions to ameliorate the adverse effects of leaving home. However, it might be the case that those depressed prior to leaving home are already exhibiting a reaction to the prospective move. By contrast those who become active and enjoy their environment seem best able to plan and to become committed to a new institution. Lack of pre-move depression may be a predictor for early adaptive behaviour as a response to change.

It has been found that previous experience of moves away to reside in an institution can ameliorate homesickness in later moves. Moves to stay with family and friends for holidays or jobs in the summer are not effective in this way. It is experience of life in an institution that seems to be the important immunizing factor. Those students who have been away to boarding school seem less likely to be adversely affected than those who have not. Equally, those students at boarding school who have been to an earlier (preparatory) boarding school are less likely to be affected by homesickness. This suggests that some immunizing process is possible.

In general, the move to university is a very difficult and demanding period for a student. Self-reported stress levels are very high. Academic work may reflect this in a number of ways; the student is likely to be absent-minded, non-attentive or to avoid lectures. This leads to a spiral of poor progress and increasing distress owing to perceived failure.

Summary

Many university students may encounter considerable stress especially if there has also been a move from home to take up residence. Principle sources of stress concern coping with the institutional and academic demands of university, study patterns, and coping with financial budgets.

6

Examination Stress

Introduction

All students have to face the demands of attaining academic standards. Proof of ability is usually tested by written examination papers or by assessment in an oral examination. Although continuous assessment plays a part its drawbacks seem to be the demand on the students to remain competent throughout the teaching year and the difficulties of staff–student relationships under these conditions.

In spite of the focus on the examination as a means of assessment there has been very little careful research in this area. All students seem to be more emotionally vulnerable at examination times. Mechanic (1966) showed that within the American post-graduate system, examinations had a profound negative effect on candidates and their families. Albas and Albas (1984) reported that students who were married were less sexually active. Student logs reported by Albas showed that nightmares, sudden mood alterations and superstitious behaviour increases as the examination approaches.

Magic and superstitious behaviour

It is hypothesized that the superstitious or 'magical' behaviour Albas reported in students prior to impending examinations is anxiety-reducing and could be seen as a coping mechanism. Main sources of student fears are assumed to be whether the question has been correctly interpreted and whether the answer will be understood by the examiners. Magical or superstitious behaviour functions to increase the chance of a positive outcome, although no logical relationship between action and outcome can be assumed to exist. Thus working hard, or trying hard might be seen to be important but does not guarantee success. Superstitious behaviour is an attempt to boost the chances of success. Locations assumed to be lucky or the carrying of mascots are argued to be part of this behaviour. It is hypothesized that there are two types of luck attitude. The materialistic approach is concerned with items of luck, whereas the behavioural approach involves rituals of a religious or secular nature, music and response to others. Trying to 'deserve' success may be an important feature of the ritual. These behaviours perhaps proliferated because control is so vicarious and is a response to stress.

Test anxiety

Test anxiety was investigated by Sarason (1972) and it was found that increased anxiety in test environments has a debilitating effect on performance. This is in keeping with the Yerkes–Dodson law described previously in that raised arousal causes performance to decrease if base levels are already at optimum or over.

Hamilton (1955) argued that one of the possible explanations of the debilitating effect of test anxiety is that it generates trains of 'internal' information or worry directed towards the likely effects of failure and that this detracts from task activity. When information generated by worrying about the test reduces the capacity available for performing the task, the result is that performance breaks down and the result becomes self confirming. Breaking the test anxiety loop is therefore very important and may indicate that examination training should be an essential ingredient of undergraduate or graduate programmes.

The failings of traditional exams

From all that has been stated above, it is clear that the traditional timed examination is likely to measure a great deal more than just the ability to acquire and utilize knowledge. It measures confidence differences, which may be age or gender based, test anxiety levels, degree of belief in superstitious practice, because this affects confidence; and ability on the day to lower anxiety sufficiently to interpret questions and set out well argued answers. Coping was more likely to result in positive affects and satisfaction. Defensive behaviour was associated with negative affect including somatic complaints (headaches, tension, feeling sick, etc.).

Additionally, social relationships during training have a marked effect on success outcome, particularly for females. Spiegel *et al.* (1986) showed that interpersonal stress was high in third- and fourth-year medical students. This of course may reflect as much as cause exam-related stress and may in any case relate to the demands of competitive endeavours. Heubner *et al.* (1981) described distrustful, non-supportive and often hostile relations between faculty members and students. Women students had higher levels of conflicts with ward sisters. Linn and Zeppa (1984) reported inverse relationships between subjective stress ratings and scores of academic performance. The role of non-cognitive factors in predicting the success rates of female medical students is argued by Spiegel *et al.* (1986) to be a significant finding (see also Willoughby *et al.* 1979).

Blumberg *et al.* (1984) found that although women were more likely to seek support from a physician, they were also likely to be able to turn anxious premonitions to advantage when faced with the examination paper. There was some indication that some forms of interpersonal stress were turned to advantage by women students in that they felt challenged by male stereotypes of women. This does not fit with other findings that suggest low confidence in females with regard to tests. Clearly some research is needed to investigate these issues. Perhaps the clue lies in the way that females seek and make use of support for their anxieties.

If all these factors are involved as outcome predictors for examinations it might be seen on first consideration to suggest that the examination process is a failure. It might, however, be countered that facility under pressure is an important test of academic ability. To mobilize information and present it in the form of detailed arguments must itself be a sign of considerable skill. At a time when knowledge acquisition is being considered to be less important than the acquisition of skills to utilize knowledge, perhaps the mobilization of available information within restricted time is a more expedient test.

Mental health and examinations

As shown in Figure 6.1 the approach of examinations has an effect in terms of psychoneurotic scores. In particular, anxiety and obsessionality scores rise in the four months prior to examinations. Following the examination diet, there is a rise in psychoneurotic scores because of increases in depression and somatic symptoms.

These results suggest that before examinations there is raised anticipatory anxiety perhaps boosted by a high work-load. After the examinations are over, there is a rise in depression scores. This may be because an event of great importance is now over and the outcome is still unknown. Poor confidence or perception of poor performance could be

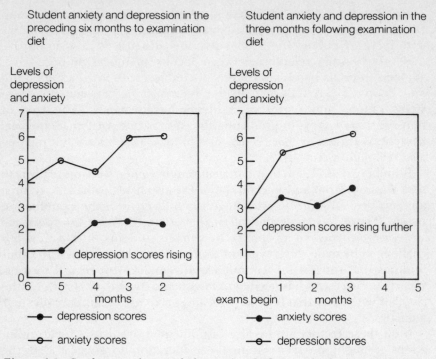

Figure 6.1 Student anxiety and depression before and after examinations: examination stress as assessed by Middlesex Hospital questionnaire

the main reason for depression after the event when no further changes are possible.

This chapter has been concerned with examination stress and its impact on students. There has been relatively little careful research on the topic in spite of its importance. What research is available suggests that examination competence and success depends on a large number of complex factors including social relationships, personal problems, gender, sense of challenge and superstitious beliefs.

Collectively, the findings suggest that some more profound aspect of ability is mobilized and that outcome reflects more than just personal knowlege. The argument that the person with a good knowledge base will best be able to withstand motivational and emotional pressures is undermined by the fact that memory characteristics change in conditions of high anxiety.

Perhaps the timed examination survives more because of its processing efficiency than for its efficiency in tapping of knowledge levels and expertise. Since considerable efforts have been made nationally in the UK to improve lecturing and communication, it seems strange that the same focus has not been given to examinations when, for some individuals, suicide is the outcome of low grades and failure.

Summary

Tests and examinations are likely to impose considerable strain on candidates. The degree of strain may reflect the level of aspiration and the consequences of failure as much as the conditions under which the examination is conducted and the level of difficulty of the paper. Prior to examination diets many students experience increasing levels of anxiety and increased sleeplessness. Following the completion of the examination diet there may be a period of increasing depression when students reflect on their performance and compare it with those of their colleagues.

More emphasis is needed on understanding the impact of examinations on students, on identifying vulnerable individuals and on the appropriateness of the current examination process.

7

Creativity and Context

Academic demands in UK universities

Academic staff in UK higher education institutions have to perform a number of roles simultaneously. They are expected to teach, meet tutorial, laboratory or seminar commitments and at the same time carry out research, run experiments, obtain research funding and write papers and books. In addition, a high public performance profile is increasingly demanded by universities seeking to enhance their reputation. In turn this means more demands on academic staff. In the UK, academics are now subject to government determined procedures in which all these various elements are listed and rated. Funding to universities and to departments within the universities reflects the outcome of these ratings.

What is outlined above is a classic example of role overload and role conflict. With so many different kinds of activity possible in a working day, the risk of overload is very high and the likelihood that one task will have to be completed at the cost of neglecting another is increased. This increases the risk of failure in one or more aspects of work.

It is likely that the most vulnerable aspect of work will be the voluntary element. The time available for research and for the care, check and preparation process which are needed for sustaining good quality output across a period of time, is less likely to be externally paced and therefore more likely to be the fuse wire of the system as student numbers increase.

Life stability and work

Processes connected with research are sensitive to stress. In studies on work and careers Vincino and Bass (1978) found that life stability, as assessed by low life stress scares, correlated with managerial success and a perception of challenge on tasks. Managers with highly stable life stress backgrounds scored higher on assessment patterns associated with job success. Two American theses have shown that life stress is negatively correlated with indices of academic performance (Harris 1972) and teaching effectiveness (Carranza 1972).

The surrounding context of work is important. Not only is there a tendency for domestic issues to spill over into the work environment (Johnson and Sarason 1979) but the availability of social support can help to offset the effects of stress and the impairment of the work role (Bhaget 1980, 1985). A number of aspects of work such as job satisfaction, organizational commitment, absenteeism and intention to leave, are sensitive to stress. Fisher and Pemberton (1992) reported high absenteeism in the Scottish Prison Service after a period of prison stress and unrest.

The finding that individuals can manage to accept work demands and respond effectively if they are supported by people around them (Schuler 1980) is important. This can be broken down into a number of key elements – admiration, respect or love for the other person; the expression of agreement and acknowledgement of the other person in terms of rights, and aid with practical help.

The problem with university environments is that competition for resources and the difficulty of being successful in a multi-role environment can create competition and hostilities that prevent cooperation and social support. The conflict between the Cambridge- and London-based research groups that was reported by Crick and Watson in the *Double Helix*, their account of the discovery of the structure of DNA, is perhaps not untypical of competitive research environments.

Recent studies of the effect of personal conflict has shown that there are major sources of stress which can easily eclipse in magnitude the more readily identified forms of work strain. Fisher and Pemberton (1993) in a survey of the Scottish Prison Service, identified interpersonal conflict as a major stress. Officers reported feeling angry if a colleague was perceived to be unfairly promoted or because of feeling let down or undermined by a colleague.

More recently, Leyman (1990) has identified the phenomena of mobbing in work environments. What begins as a conflict with a superior can easily become an uncontrolled process leading to isolation. If the superior discriminates and leaves that person out of decision making, the result can be that colleagues perceive a loser and avoid contact. The character of the victim may then change in favour of suspicion and paranoia and eventually a run-down process is initiated.

These factors have not yet been made explicit in academic environments but Leyman quotes the case of an individual researcher treated in
this way. Heads of departments may be untrained and unsuited for the
power they can wield.

Factors that affect research productivity

Statistical evidence on productivity factors

Over (1982) has investigated some of the statistical data on productivity
in academics and has made a number of findings of interest. Using a
cross-sectional design, Over (1982) obtained data on publication rates of
psychologists between 1968 and 1970 and from 1978 to 1980 for
different age groups. Scientists appointed in 1970 published more
frequently from 1968 to 1970 than from 1978 to 1980. However,
although productivity dropped with age, publication rates from 1978 to
1980 were better predicted by previous publication rates from 1968 to
1970 than by age, moreover 56 per cent of those studied and categorized
on the basis of early productivity levels did not change in status over the
ten-year period. Over's data showed that 26 per cent published nothing
at either the first or second time of measurement, 17 per cent
maintained medium productivity and 13 per cent were highly productive. Approximately 23.8 per cent of the variance in publication rate
could be explained as a function of past productivity; a further 6.6 per
cent of the variance was attributable to university affiliation. By
comparison with these variables age, sex and level of appointment did
not exert a significant influence.

The study also showed that British psychologists who were over 45
published less than their colleagues who were under 45, which is argued
by Over to be consistent with the view that research achievement peaks
by the end of the fourth decade. Slippage in time from productive to
non-productive status seems to be characteristic of the groups studied.
Over points out that the trend towards retaining older individuals in
posts that is typical of the British university system will mean that
research productivity decreases. However, the existence of a number of
older more productive individuals can help to offset this and if
appointments by productivity are made and retirement policies changed
this might counteract the effects.

One issue of importance is whether age is a factor that influences the
impact of research publications. It has been claimed that scientists
become less creative as they become older. A British mathematician cited
by Over (1988) asserts that mathematics is a young man's game and that

he knew of no instance of a major mathematical advance by a man past 50 and that if anyone over 50 lost interest in the subject there would be no great loss (see also Hardy 1967). Einstein is cited by Over as having said that a person who has not made his contribution to science by the age of 30 will never do so.

Lehman (1953) found data to support the idea that age and achievement indices are negatively correlated. Using data from histories of science to identify outstanding achievement it was found that the majority of discoveries are made by individuals under the age of 40. Interestingly, there were differences between subjects in this respect. The peak age for achievement ranged from 26 to 30 for chemistry, and from 36 to 40 for genetics, physiology, geology and psychology. Lehman's conclusions are that highly frequent publishing can occur beyond the age of 40 but what is produced is likely to have less impact. Creativity is assumed to rise to maximum in the 30s and then to fall off slowly. However, the above point about age and subject area must be considered.

In describing Lehman's work Over points out that Lehman's study does not allow for differences in the numbers of scientists in each age group and makes the legitimate point that he should have asked whether the proportion of scientists making a contribution at each age category differed. Lehman argues that in Zuckermann's study of the age distribution of Nobel Prize winners, the majority were young at the time of their discovery. However, when allowance is made for the number of scientists at different ages, the effect is lost.

One problem with these investigations involving performance indices is the difficulty of obtaining an effective measure of productivity. Citation indices generally lag behind and authors may be frequently cited in cases where three is poor data or faulty methodology. Over attempted a study based on data from one of the most prestigious journals for psychologists, *The Psychological Review*. Although most articles in this journal were published by young authors this could be predicted by number imbalance. On a cross-sectional analysis, this effect was minimized and there was no difference between older and younger authors in terms of mean citation rates. Older authors were no less likely than younger authors to have generated a high impact article. Citation rates do, however, include poor research output because authors may criticize poor work.

Gender differences in publication levels

An issue of importance is that men and women have been shown to differ markedly in their promotion prospects at university. A study by

Over and Lancaster (1984) examined gender differences in the context of the four disciplinary groupings of the Australian university system (behavioural science, education, humanities, social science) from 1962 to 1964 and 1975 to 1976. Proportionately more men than women gained promotion. In the first cohort studied, 68 per cent of men but only 30 per cent of women were lecturers within seven years of appointment. For the second cohort, 48 per cent of men and 30 per cent of women were promoted. Statistical results showed that the likelihood of promotion varied with gender when allowance was made for research output and for level and place of qualification.

Over and Lancaster argued that it was difficult to understand the process by which the gender effect operates, but quoted a survey carried out by the Federation of Australian University Staff Association in which women reported that, compared with their male counterparts, they had received unfavourable treatment on appointment, promotion, tenure and study leave. However, the study was based only on reporting differences and the women who were involved differed in discipline, qualification, specialization, rank and age from male counterparts.

Over (1982) suggested that one test of whether discrimination occurred was whether women who gained academic posts were better qualified than their male counterparts. He compared 608 men and 608 women matched in pairs for university affiliation, discipline and level of appointment and found no difference within the Australian system.

The possibility that entry requirements do not distinguish men from women but career development patterns do, was also not found to be tenable. Emmons (1982) investigated the 'revolving door' phenomenon whereby entrance qualifications are the same for women and men but women are more likely to be passed over for promotion. Emmons found no evidence for this either in terms of holding an appointment over time, or in terms of promotion to associate professor in seven years. Women were no more likely than men to have migrated to a lower-status university.

However, discriminatory practices against females have been established within the American university system. Between 1960 and 1970 women who had gained doctorates from top-ranking departments and had published as much as men had lower salaries on average and were less likely to have gained recognition in terms of rank and tenure (Zuckermann and Cole, in Over 1980). One possible explanation is that women are reluctant to pursue success; another is that they may avoid the rigours of an interview panel when the chances of success are perceived as low because of an all-male panel.

Although in terms of holding a doctorate on appointment women were better than men, the average number of papers published per year was 0.49 by female psychologists and 0.84 by male psychologists and the difference was significant (Over 1980). Men were likely to be sole authors of 50 per cent of the papers published and women were sole authors on 49.1 per cent of occasions. The difference in publication rates may reflect the dual role of women in that rearing children even with back-up services may create overload.

Sensitivity of research productivity to context

Clearly more work is needed on how and why academics become productive in research. The evidence suggests that, if anything, once productive an academic tends to stay productive and this in general sustains against slippage downwards due to age. Perhaps career patterns are being established which become stabilized. Those who give research priority may gain intrinsic regards that tend to increase their focus in this direction – creativity breeds success, which reinforces further creativity.

As outlined previously, life-style factors and contexts may be the dominant factors in dictating the form and nature of productivity. The effect on females is particularly interesting in that, although often reported as being better qualified than men in terms of doctoral qualifications, they generally produce fewer papers on average. This could be less a function of ability than of factors such as lack of time because of other distractions.

The role of women in work environments has been well explained by Stewart and Salt (1981) and their results suggest that working women who are married generally fare better in terms of well-being and health than those at home in traditional roles and those who are single and work. However, the time required for academic work may not be available to women. In fact Stewart and Salt account for their results in terms of a 'buffer' hypothesis: women at work who are married offset the pressures of work against the pressures of home. They do not have the time to be equally worried about both and this leads them to be rather more immunized from stress.

Defocusing because of multiple roles may be beneficial in many ways but may hit productivity rather harder. Research involving the setting up and completion of experiments or the analysis of events from manuscripts and books is a time consuming process and may only be accomplished by the single-minded male who does not have multiple roles to fulfil. Also, as described earlier, multiple roles create additional stress and switching between tasks is highly stressful.

The importance of stable life contexts, life-style practices and role definition in terms of domestic or work commitments may be important determinants of career and promotion prospects at university. Lack of promotion and status across age may in the end determine stress in work environments.

Summary

Life circumstances have been found to affect creative processes in academics and to reduce productivity. This may be a particular problem that needs exploring for both academic staff and students. A number of personal circumstances have been identified as factors that influence productivity. For example there are differences between males and females and a reduction in productivity with age. Females in general have career profiles that rarely achieve senior status in spite of having equal impact of research papers in journals of merit. Some of the possible reasons for this concern the mechanisms of promotion. If women are judged by panels which are predominately male, there may be an inclination to assume that the chances of selection will be lower. This then may influence a female candidate against attending for interview. The same argument might be true for promotion panels.

8

Stress in Academic Staff

Financial cuts and reduction of personal control

As outlined in earlier chapters, research on occupational stress has emphasized that when the demand made on a person is high but personal discretion or jurisdiction is also high, the result is that the demand is seen as a challenge. A positive experience is likely even if workload is raised. Conversely, when demand is high but discretion or control is low, the result can be negative, leading to distress. This is the essence of the job strain model first proposed by Karasek (1979). Competitive pressures in situations of limited financial resources will change the nature of the task faced by a workforce. When the change occurs as a result of financial cuts increased demand on individuals may be accompanied by an erosion of control.

Academic staff have enjoyed a number of unusual features of employment, many of which have in the past been consonant with the notion of high personal control. Their conditions of employment and hours of work allowed for great flexibility. They could operate in a number of different spheres of activity, including teaching, research and administration, often at self-determined times. There are now identifiable constraints on choice of activity, however. A specified number of lectures, tutorials, and laboratory sessions must be given, for instance. There is the pressure not only of teaching more students but also of obtaining funding for research. More time has to be spent in preparing applications for funding of research activity. As information density increases and more time is required, so perceived overload rises.

The demands on academics have risen rapidly over the last ten years. In theory the freedom indicative of high control still exists, but in practice there has been a steady erosion of job control. All the signs are that this will continue.

As already outlined in the first chapter, Kogan and Kogan (1983) argued that the funding cuts were expenditure led and that the attempt to justify the cuts was a later preoccupation. Dr Rhodes Boyson maintained that cutting higher education would have positive benefits (Kogan and Kogan 1983: 12) but in general the government appeared to have very little idea of the consequences of their action and little by way of an overall plan. A plan for no plan was apparent. Kogan and Kogan point out that government policies began in ignorance and confusion over policies remained typical of successive years.

Kogan and Kogan note that the government made its cuts first by increasing overseas students fees, which had the effect of withdrawing financial support, and then by a further 8.5 per cent cut implying a cumulative 13 per cent across three years. This was in addition to the 10 per cent of income lost per student in the 1970s. According to Kogan and Kogan the UGC were left to work out the detailed consequences. The decision was made to preserve staffing ratios in order to continue with research, so universities had to reduce student intake. A form of low control was imposed on universities in that jurisdiction on managerial decisions was reduced.

Kogan and Kogan further make the point that although cuts began as an expenditure-led exercise, the justification for the cuts was then taken up by government ministers. Sir Keith Joseph focused on the social sciences, reducing the budgets, arguing that higher education, he believed, should be seen as part of a market economy, presumably as subject as any other aspect of the economy to financial and competitive pressure.

Clearly these processes have had direct consequences for the universities. Although a 1981 White Paper emphasized the need to support basic science, undermining the fabric of support for laboratories and teaching resources had the opposite effect. Research capacity was inevitably endangered.

What is perhaps more important is that universities with low levels of fees and block grants could not support research and development for the pump priming initiatives needed as a basis for funding applications to the research councils. Seen in this light, the universities lost control to central sources. The Government operates a parental role in dictating via the Funding Council what can actually occur. Passing on restrictions by evolving a formula for funding departments implants reduced control at the individual level by determining basic pressure level and how time should be spent. Social pressure forces individuals to carry out research and encourages them to seek funds for doing so. Whilst some might argue that this is why academics are in existence, the impact on those who cannot come up with viable ideas can be great.

Other forms of low control evolved as the impact of the cuts and the breadth of government influence developed further. For example, the research councils decided to award penalties for dissertations not in on time or not completed. This puts pressure on a supervisor to approve work as suitable for submission just so that further grants can be obtained. Control over quality and the necessary judgements a supervisor should make, are lost.

Another example of the erosion of control for academics is the demands made by extra student numbers. The control over teaching practice and timetable content is eroded when student numbers are increased, unless staff–student ratios are stabilized by extra funds. Even so, specialist areas still have to be covered and the creation of an extra teaching post may not even out demand in specific teaching areas.

Stress in academics

Against the above background this chapter focuses on the results of studies conducted to investigate aspects of stress in academic staff in British universities and colleges. The studies inevitably involve short term sampling of different time intervals. Any study of occupational stress necessarily involves a snapshot of the life of the workforce. The sampling process does not involve repeated measures on the same groups because of changes in employment, etc. and because the need for anonymous returns makes recording names impossible.

Background to the reported studies

The first study conducted in 1988, was carried out at a time when universities were under considerable pressure. Cuts were being imposed, there was high uncertainty about present and future. Faculty boards and deans met to consider possible loss of staff or even in some cases complete departments. Small departments and those non-productive in research were likely targets for cuts and closures. In some cases administrators or senior academic staff interviewed those who had low research profiles.

It is inevitable that as funds to the research councils are cut, the probability of grant funding decreases even for high grade proposals for research. At the same time with universities desperate for funds, the pressure was increased to apply for grants. Gradually during the 1980s, creativity and productivity became essential features of academic life. The cost of failure could be high in terms of social approval and self esteem – researchers who were able; and perhaps lucky, became the élite of departments. They were more likely to be given good facilities and to have a more influential say in policy.

Some academics believe that cartels operate so that those in the favoured groups have the chance to be reviewers and assessors and thus to have a better chance of getting to know about critical funding initiatives.

B. E. Skinner once noted that whilst it was easy enough to explain reinforced (or rewarded) behaviour, it was always more difficult to explain unreinforced activity. The human propensity to persist with behaviour that has a low chance of reward defies simple analysis, yet is an implicit aspect of academic staff survival. Evidence suggests that some academics become depressed at having carefully prepared proposals turned down. We have now collected a small sample of individual cases where this was a definite result. The impact for some staff can be reluctance to continue with grant applications.

The research councils, also operating under pressure, did not consider the broader issues. Grants could be turned down without any feedback, or eminent researchers could receive a stylized letter in which the phrase 'not up to standard' was present in some form. This bland, negative dismissal followed grant preparations that often involved over 50 hours of work and at a time when the pressure for success was high.

It would seem to be a poor managerial strategy to create such unrewarding work conditions. Work demand is high and control over outcome very low. A crude analogy to what happened to the universities in this period would be that of a group of athletes attempting to win a race over an obstacle course while wearing leg fetters.

Remembering the assertions of Kogan and Kogan that the cuts were expenditure-led rather than being based on productivity or quality assessments, the work situation facing academics had all the qualities likely to produce stress, frustration and low self-esteem. Good quality, alpha-rated projects are still incurring high levels of rejections from the research councils and charities and few attempts to make initial decisions based on short outlines are evident.

Finally, the lack of back up for academics has meant that many staff were coping with overload in three areas – teaching, research and administration. Role overload is a major source of stress at work and such conditions encourage failure. It is impossible to work effectively when human resources are overloaded. Laboratory research has shown that when a human being attempts to cope with a main task (such as driving a car) and is asked to complete a secondary task such as tapping or calling out random numbers, the ability to sustain the rates of output without pause, error or breakdown is affected as the demands of the first task increase.

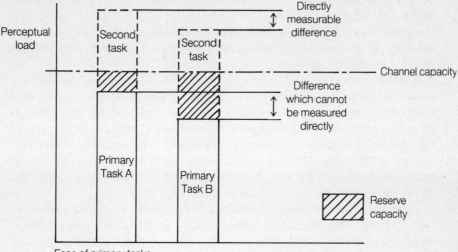

Figure 8.1   Mental load in two different tasks

Figure 8.1 illustrates the conceptual formulations of the way in which two tasks can be compared in terms of their mental load by assessing the level of performance on an added 'secondary task'. A difficult main task reduces the available resources for performance of a secondary task. The loss of competence on a secondary task thus provides a basic index of limitations on human capacity. As demands rise, capacity may be increased but capacity is itself finite and when the ceiling is reached overload occurs and the performance on a secondary task breaks down and errors occcur.

Lack of back-up resources for academics inevitably means that several tasks run currently in a fixed period of time. It would be anticipated that performance is less than optimum on all of them. As outlined previously, time sharing between tasks implies constant interruption, which is also stressful. Mandler and Watson (1966) demonstrated raised arousal in situations of interruption. Most senior executives with busy offices and work schedules, especially when they include external commitments, can expect personal secretarial support. A secretary is not only necessary to cope with mail and telephone calls but also protects an executive against overload by scheduling his or her diary to avoid sudden interruptions.

Academic staff, even those of great reputation, often lack this protection. The ratio of office staff to academic staff varies but there are many situations where two secretaries service up to fourteen staff. As productivity levels and interactions with outside institutes increase, the ability of secretarial staff to cope with academic needs decreases. Academics faced with tasks such as lecturing, research, writing research grant applications and organizing administrative tasks, are potentially in overload situations.

They may also have to create their own filing systems, type their own work, prepare their own reports and fix their own appointments and travel arrangements. Additionally, they are potentially exposed to demands of the needs of undergraduate and postgraduate students and the potential demand on them to deal with personal problems and academic difficulties. If staff–student ratios are over 17, the demand on staff can potentially be very high in terms of lecture contact time and 'hourage' spent coping with student demands.

One impact of the financial cuts has been to create funding pressures and lack of administrative support. This in turn has the effect of reducing personal jurisdiction. Additionally, uncertainty and perceived lack of plans for the future of the university creates conditions of anxiety (plans for no plans are likely to enhance insecurity).

Finally, the public image of academic staff has not been encouraging. They often have to act as consultants for people earning double and triple their own salaries. The occurrence of the poorly-paid expert is common in the academic world and should be rectified if the new higher education system of the year 2000 is to be viable. The assumption that academics do little work is not substantiated by the facts but appears to have become an established view. It may be that academics themselves have never been effective lobbyists for their own position because of the varied nature of their own group composition.

Problems with the assessment of occupational stress

One of the problems involved in any occupational stress study is that use of a control group whilst desirable, is difficult. Both self-selection and work selection factors are likely to differentiate work groups because of personal attractions and interests and the selection imposed by those who make the decisions about acceptability of candidates for jobs.

Use of a 'matched' control group may create unknown major difficulties because there is very little research on what the important matching factors should be. In the case of academic staff it is not clear whether they should be compared with general sedentary intelligent populations or specifically with Civil Service scientists, bank managers and executives, with secondary school teachers, or business administrators. In the study described here, it was decided to use normative data where possible at least initially. The norms for the general population formed the basis for comparison.

A second problem concerns the influence of personal control on the scheduling of work activity for those with relatively high personal jurisdiction. Although it has been argued that control has been reduced for academics as a result of the cuts, it remains the case that they have a great deal of discretion over the way they organize their time, where to work, the order in which deadlines are to be met, the treatment of students, etc. Overall, however, pressures to be successful and bring money in to the university, whether by research or by increased student numbers, lead to control being eroded. Adjustments may be made by identifying priorities and evolving different 'targets' or personal goals. Fisher (1989) argues that different control targets need to be identified in more detail in the work environment. Personal targets determine work priorities, which in turn determine the sorts of stress that occur. High personal control over demands of the academic task may imply a more restricted range of targets.

Assessment of occupational staff in terms of levels of academic stress

The study involved assessing levels of psychological distress scores in a random selection of academics at two randomly chosen universities in Scotland. Staff were assessed for psychological health, absent-mindedness and personally perceived problems and associated worry levels. The Middlesex Hospital Questionnaire was used to assess levels of psychoneurotic symptoms. The diagnostic is useful because it does not require symptoms to be predicted in advance. It affords an overall score indicating levels of distress and a breakdown into subscale scores on anxiety, depression, obsessionality, phobias, somatic symptoms (concern with health and physical symptoms) and hysteria.

The study also involved asking academics to complete a weekly diary of problems and associated hours of worry. As indicated in Chapter 1 this is consistent with a technique developed by Fisher and Elder (1991) that assumes that an epidemiology of work stress can be established for different work groups. The approach has the advantage that there is no prejudging of the problem content in terms of whether or not it would be characterized by independent observers as stressful. The subject makes this decision in identifying a particular event to report. The data provided are quantitative in terms of the average number of problems per person per week, and qualitative in terms of the problem content.

Academic staff were sampled by means of applying a table of random

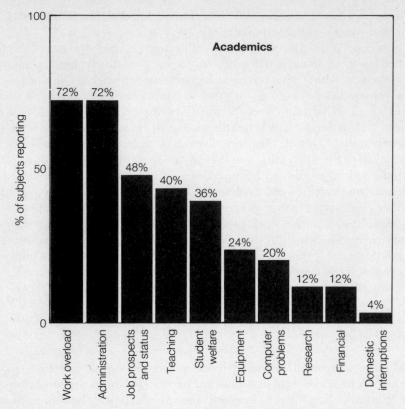

Figure 8.2a   Classified problem categories based on problems of academics

numbers to staff lists in the diary. Those not in post, on sabbatical leave or retired were not involved in the study. Those absent due to illness received their booklets at home.

Returns, made via the internal mail or the postage system, averaged 85 per cent. There was an expected but unfortunate gender ratio in that 78 males and 7 females took part in the study. Given the imbalance of males to females in university such an effect would be expected.

MHQ scores overall could not be compared with norms for the test because published data on these are not available from the test's authors or in publication. However, normative data has been collected for the subscale scores and on statistical analysis academics were found to rank higher in both anxiety, depression and obsessionality scores than the general population. This confirms that psychological stress is a feature of occupational life for academics as assessed by a snapshot through time in the summer of 1988.

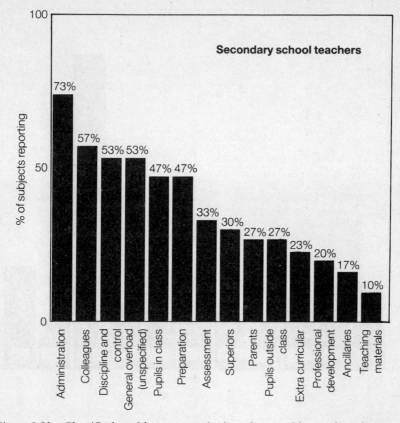

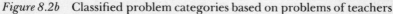

Figure 8.2b   Classified problem categories based on problems of teachers

Analysis of the number of problems reported in the individual diaries showed that there was an average of 7 work problems per person per week out of a potential total of 21. Unfortunately there are no established norms for comparison. Prison officers in a recent study conducted in the Scottish prisons, reported average levels of 14 per person per week. Figure 8.2 shows that when the content of problems was analysed in detail and classified using three judges and 100 per cent agreement, the main sources of work problems concern overload, administrative load, job status and teaching.

Figure 8.3 illustrates the worry levels associated with particular problems reported. Worry levels are obtained by counting the number of hours per day that the subject recalls being worried by a particular problem. Thus some measure of the 'mind-grabbing' quality of a particular problem can be identified albeit on only crude measure. The

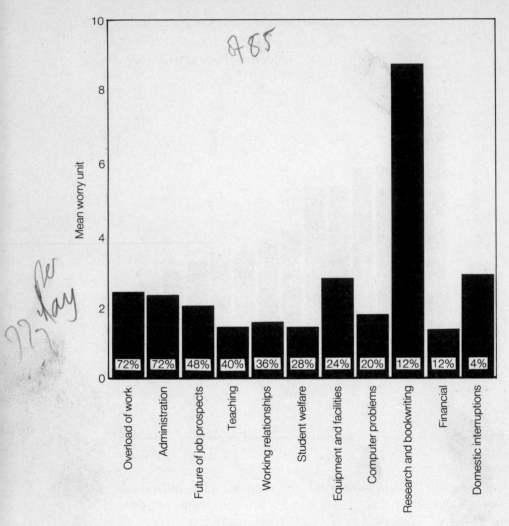

Figure 8.3   Worry levels associated with daily problems (The mean worry level of each problem category indicates the number of hour units in which a respondent recalls being worried or strongly concerned.)

preoccupation with a stressful problem probably reflects its intensity, frequency or probability of occurrence.

Figure 8.3 reveals an interesting effect when compared with Figure 8.2. Although only 12 per cent of the academics who took part in the study reported problems concerned with research, the average worry

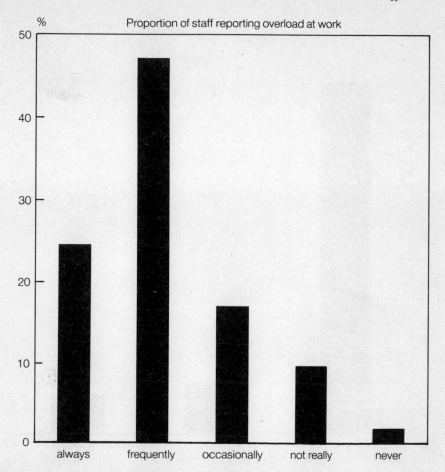

Figure 8.4 1992 survey of academic staff perceived overload

level for research related problems is very high. Thus we have low percentage report, but high worry characteristics concerned with research problems. This is very similar to personal health problems where frequency in the population is low but intensity as assessed by worry frequency is high.

One possible explanation of this is that at the time of the study few academics were engaging in research. However, for those who were, a high degree of worry and distress was associated with it. This may suggest that research activity is only carried out when other work and environmental conditions are congenial and that when it is, the levels of worry and concern are high.

A second study carried out in a randomly selected university

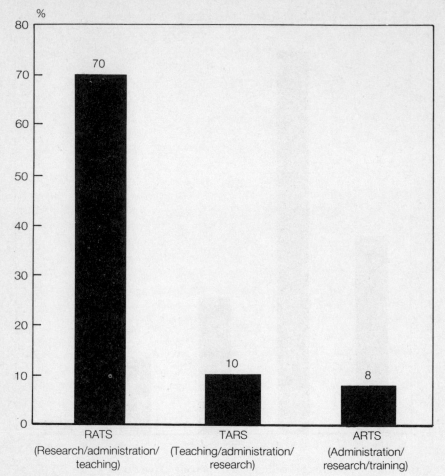

%

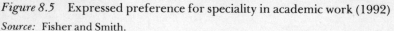

Figure 8.5   Expressed preference for speciality in academic work (1992)
Source: Fisher and Smith.

confirmed the results of the previous study in identifying overload as a
major factor in the lives of academic staff at all status levels, from
lecturing to professorial staff.

Figure 8.4 shows that 75 per cent of staff report experiencing
overload 'always' or 'frequently'. This particular study was conducted
(Fisher and Smith 1993) at a time when research activity was being rated
continuously by departments, faculties and universities. Under these
circumstances the option of leaving research activity to cope with more
pressing demands will have been changed by what is in effect a new
pay-off structure.

Figure 8.5 illustrates a finding from the same group of subjects which shows that when asked about preferred use of time over 70 per cent of academics sampled indicated they would prefer to be engaged in research. This finding may reflect not only the creative needs of those who become academics but also the new pressures on academics in terms of the rewards for research that filter down from the funding systems that dictate the value of research.

Summary

Academic staff have had to endure expenditure-led cuts in funding and a growth in student numbers. This has meant that inevitably there is reduction in control over features of the work environment. Practices that depend on judgements of quality may no longer be appropriate in situations where universities are in need of funding. Overload and particularly role overload emerge as the main features of the self-reported stressful problems of academics. Most academics, when asked, indicate that they would prefer to spend time in research activity.

9

Overload and Division of Labour

The problems of overload

One approach to the issue of perceived stress in working environments is to focus on what the workforce report as stressful problems. Categorizing of problems by independent judges provides an indication of principal sources of problem. The previous chapter shows that the major source of problems are concerned with overload and administration problems.

Overload is likely to be a direct cause of stress because high density of activity in a limited period of time is intrinsically over-arousing and creates biological states characterized by raised heart rate, blood pressure and high cholesterol levels. A study of tax accountants in the USA showed that as the tax year end approached their serum cholesterol levels increased. Deadlines imposed by the tax year were identified as key determinants of the effect (Friedman *et al.* 1958).

Academics will experience deadline stress when grant applications or faculty papers have to be prepared, and when lecture classes and tutorials are scheduled. These events will form part of external pacing that could be likened to having to meet deadlines or to assembly-line work. Perhaps academics could be regarded for much of their working week as 'mental' assembly-line workers but with some control over the ordering of tasks.

Figure 8.4 has already shown that on a recent survey of 53 academics randomly sampled 75 per cent reported overload as happening 'always' or 'frequently'.

Role overload

One aspect of overload is that brought about by the carrying out of several roles simultaneously. An academic is both a teacher, researcher, organizer and administrator. The relative balance of these comparative tasks has not been formally investigated and is likely to vary between individuals and institutions. Switching from task to task is biologically arousing.

Additionally, interruption increases the risk of failure in that when a person is focusing on one task, the other is likely to be left. This risks error or failure in at least one domain. One lecturer wrote that he was so busy trying to get a grant application in on the deadline (it required 50 hours of work beforehand) that he completely forgot about a lecture he was due to give. Over 40 students waited for over 25 minutes before complaining.

The research literature on personal control would suggest that academics should function best when they are able to organize a sequence of events such as meetings or classes. Timetables compiled by university committees ahead of the academic year often leave little possibility of adjustments to ease periods of overload. The only self-determined elements may be personal research periods and this may mean that research is neglected because it becomes the 'fuse-wire' of the system when load is high.

Mass higher education in line with Europe is likely to exacerbate the problem because of the increase in teaching density it involves. Methods of streamlining teaching have not yet evolved to keep track of these new demands. Tutorial classes may still be offered to large numbers of first- and second-year students in some universities and under these conditions the load on academic staff is markedly increased. Labour intensive processes may have to be abandoned in such a high density system.

Means of reducing the overload may be found through research into alternative teaching methods but this may be slow to take effect. Use of video and film material for lectures may enable students to see 'star' performers in their fields but learning may suffer if the live theatre of lectures disappears altogether. A compromise arrangement of some recorded 'star' or 'guest' lecturers might be a helpful way of subsidizing load, although this may be expensive.

Division of labour: RATs, TARs and ARTs

Division of labour is an obvious solution to overload. The idea that there may be personal factors that create specializations, implies that there is a possibility for reducing the overload and the time spent dividing attention between disparate tasks. Figure 8.5 has already shown how a sample of 53 university academics, would prefer to spend their time

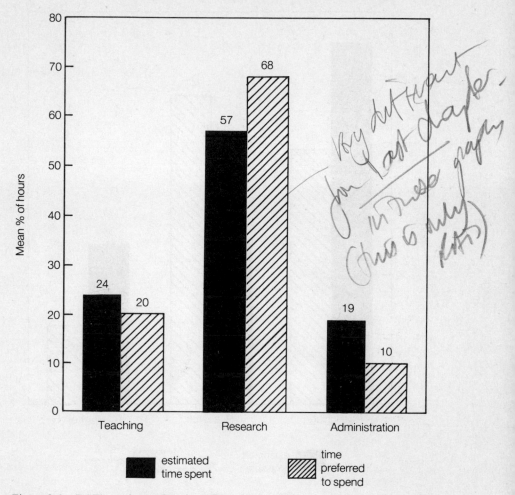

Figure 9.1 RATs: estimated and preferred speciality

each week. When asked to indicate preference 70 per cent of academics sampled listed research first and teaching or administration second. These people are termed RATs because research is dominant (RTAs are included). Ten per cent indicated that they would like to be predominantly teachers (TARs), and only a remaining 8 per cent indicated that they would like to be administrators.

This analysis of expressed preferences is not a good indicator of the potential for reducing overload by natural division of labour because too many appear to favour research profiles. However, the career structure that exists favours high research profiles because promotions are made

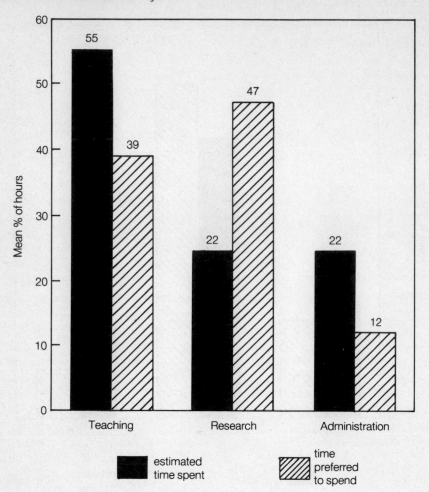

Figure 9.2   TARs: estimated and preferred speciality

on this basis. A change in career structure might influence these decisions differently. Research in the area of person–environment fit suggests that an individual must 'fit' or be compatible with the work environment (Fisher 1985). A negative fit (a mismatch) means raised job strain and decreased satisfaction at work. In turn there are implications for lowered efficiency and poor health (Fisher 1989).

Imposing research on teachers, high teaching loads on researchers, or high administration loads on either, will increase poor person–environment fit. Since individuals generally use what control they have to reduce demands that are disliked, thereby reducing stress, areas where there is little potential for control may be sacrificed. For example, if high teaching loads are enforced, use administrative short cuts, or failure to initiate scholarly activity and research may be the outcome.

Figure 9.1 shows that those designated RATs estimate that they spend about 24 per cent of their working hours on teaching and would prefer to bring this down to 20 per cent. They would prefer an increase in research time from 57 to 68 per cent and a decrease in administrative time from 19 to 10 per cent.

Figure 9.2 shows that those designated TARs have considerably higher teaching loads: 55 per cent of their time is spent in teaching. They would like it reduced to 39 per cent, which is still much higher than a researcher would prefer. 'Teachers' have a roughly similar administrative load to researchers and would like to reduce it to about the same level.

Figure 9.3 shows that ARTs have high administrative loads (53 per cent of time) and would prefer to reduce it to about 28 per cent. This is still over twice the amount researchers and teachers would wish to spend on administration.

The important point is that it is only in the area of research that all groups would want to see an increase – about 10 per cent for RATs, 20 per cent for TARs and 20 per cent for ARTs. The possible reasons for this are numerous. First, as has already been argued career structures currently favour research activity, this after all is how the subject is advanced. Second, however, research activity is less externally paced and has a greater element of personal control. As argued previously, the individual is likely to use control when it is available to influence demands made. Changing the amount of time spent in research or tutorials is one way of achieving reduction of load. Short circuiting administrative tasks is likely to generate more future problems.

Person–environment fit

A mistfit between desired and actual work demands is likely to result in stress and dissatisfaction. The possibility that overload can be reduced by division of labour, with a career structure and pay structure favouring all three domains of endeavour, would seem to be a natural answer. However, the recent research reported in this chapter suggests that at face value, research and scholarly activity are the most desired pursuits. Only RATs therefore have a reasonable chance of person–environment fit.

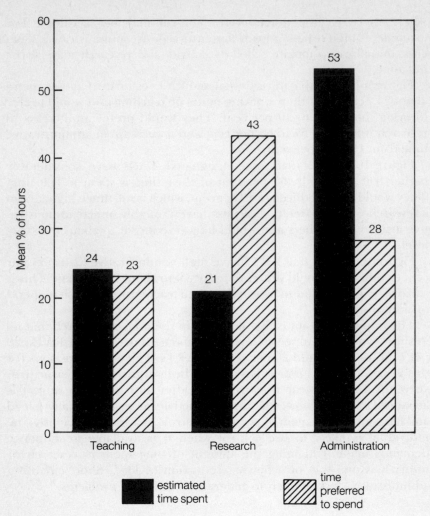

Figure 9.3   ARTs: estimated and preferred speciality

The rise and fall of knowledge

Maximizing research activity provides a level of status and excellence not easily accorded to teachers and administrators. The selectivity exercises occurring at four-year intervals in the UK maximize the need for research and its impact because funding to universities and departments depends on it. This means that research will inevitably proliferate. The background literature relevant to any research endeavour is now so substantial that the time that must be spent in coping with the existing body of knowledge about a subject area may add to the level of overload in academics. Thus academics will need more time for research, whether it is for submitting grant applications or for the writing of papers and articles. Given that academics are reporting overload already adjustments may be needed.

Knowledge mountains and thought lakes

Some parallels may be drawn with the production of food in the European Community countries. Inevitably increased efficiency leads to butter mountains and wine lakes. Perhaps, flippantly, similar processes are at work in the production and refinement of knowledge. Vast untapped reservoirs of knowledge fill the libraries and the vital progress being made is perhaps hidden by less important information accumulating and obscuring fundamental facts. There are also more journals and more need for more journals as research productivity proliferates. The journals are responsible for maintaining quality but there is pressure on journal editors to produce volumes on time and with reasonable coverage.

Using the analogy of the European Community again, perhaps there should be a method of controlling knowledge proliferation. The concept of 'set-aside land' (land deliberately not in use) has been introduced to deal with excess production. Perhaps 'set-aside' academics are needed to curb and control knowlege mountains and thought lakes. Although this suggestion is not to be taken too seriously, perhaps a way of curbing the excess of poor quality research is to implement quality control so that only some individuals seen by colleagues to have good ideas that have not been investigated will be allowed to undertake research activity and the outcome will be reviewed. Other academics might be rewarded by a lighter load, because of lack of research. A set-aside sabbatical that carries no penalty but that takes an academic off the treadmill and rewards past endeavours with 'rests' that are not necessarily deployed in teaching might be a useful approach. It is important not to lose the natural ebb and flow of the creative process in the life of academics because this process appears natural to good quality creative activity.

This system, strange as it may seem, might better mirror a natural productivity system, with the ebb and flow of natural cycles of creativity being used to drive the research output. At the moment the reported overload in academic staff and the proliferation of knowledge, often without reference to quality control, are producing knowledge gluts and academics with job strain. An ingredient of job strain is level of personal

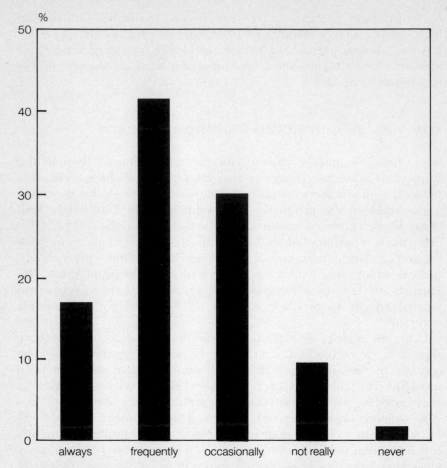

Figure 9.4   Self-perceived involvement of academics in departmental decision-making

control, and academics in general appear to have lower levels of control than is ideal.

Figure 9.4 illustrates that an unexpectedly high proportion of academics feel that they do not have much involvement in departmental decision making. Whether by personal taste or because of political factors, academics may be existing in a state of low control at work. This has implications for the levels of stress they experience and also for their capacity to influence the situations that give rise to overload. If professional and senior posts are removed then nearly all staff report very low influence.

Summary

Possible methods of dealing with overload in academics have been outlined. The idea is considered of a division of labour between staff who favour spending most of their time in research (RATs) and those who favour teaching (TARs) or administration (ARTs). The difficulty in implementing such a division of labour is that it appears that most staff will opt for research. This would mean that division of labour would be forced rather than tapping into personal inclinations. Secondly the enthusiasm of committed and creative researchers might result in better quality of lectures. Teaching-only staff might find it more difficult to be aware of state of the art content or to provide the back-up or the breadth of knowledge that supports good lectures.

10

Coping with Stress in Academics

Coping strategies

Most researchers identify two main approaches to coping strategies. The first is problem-focused coping, which involves analysis of the main sources of difficulty with a view to seeing whether changes are possible. For example a person distressed at work because of personal difficulties in the office might benefit from being moved to another location to work with a different group. Implementing problem-focused changes is a way of achieving control over the problem.

The second approach is emotion-focused; the problem cannot be solved so the person suffering distress is encouraged to try to reduce the emotional trauma; this could be seen as a damage limitation approach. The difficulty with using only an emotion-focused strategy is that the problem is never tackled and may cause further distress. Nevertheless for stresses such as bereavement, assault and trauma following major life events such as job loss, emotion-focused coping may, at least initially, be the only viable approach.

A general point of importance is that coping strategies may change the nature of the situation in many ways, some of which may be negative. Schonpflug (1989) illustrated the point by the example of a person dealing with the fact that his or her house was on fire by having the wall pulled down to extinguish the flames. He or she is then faced with a house that is no longer on fire but is missing a wall. Faulty coping strategies can become further sources of stress. It has been suggested that major states of distress may have been fuelled by coping attempts.

The problem-focused approach for academics

As outlined in previous chapters, academics seem to be faced with stress as a result of their increased workload. Switching between tasks often creates agitation if one task has to be sorted out before another is completed. Research in California has identified the adverse affects of interruption both on susbequent task performance and on mood state. Mandler (1975) proposed that 'interruption theory' could account for irritation and high arousal, which in the end might make a person tired and prone to error.

The exercise of multiple tasks involves a high level of interruption and a person rapidly enters a no-win situation in which effort and success may be expended on one task at the expense of another which is neglected. An academic desperate to meet a grant deadline, for example may find that the demands of teaching for the week are being neglected.

The problem-focused approach demands, obviously, that the problem should be addressed. At the risk of repeating some of the previous chapter, one of the important decisions might be to try for load reduction by examining what is required of academics. An obvious first approach is to see what bureaucratic elements could be removed. Universities, like all institutions are capable of generating massive amounts of paperwork. How much paperwork is necessary for the efficient running of a university has never been determined. It is almost certain that the system over-indulges. An important freedom could be gained for academics if they themselves would create a less burdensome system.

The possibility of division of labour between researchers, teachers and administrators whilst having obvious appeal seems to have difficult elements. First, as shown in the previous chapter, a high proportion of academics wish to spend more time in research. It would appear that teaching and administration are regarded as chores by comparison. This is not to devalue either teaching or administration but the repetitive nature of these activities and the constant externally-paced load might be part of the lack of attractiveness. Also as already outlined, both career structure and self-assessed confidence are more likely to be buoyant when research ideas and feedback are perceived positively.

However, it should also be borne in mind that research activity in the current climate of lack of funds, high pressure to publish, and relatively poor promotion prospects may have many negative features. The survey data nevertheless indicate that academics seem to want to do it.

A possibility not yet explored is that academics might opt for a balance of research, teaching or administration on appointment. They would then have a career structure that takes account of progress within a particular balance. However, the critical points above are not dealt with by such an approach. The current selectivity exercises do provide the possibility for division of labour and with subject research/teaching/administration balances, but the overall effect has not yet been evaluated.

Emotion-focused coping

This assumes that the work problems remain stressful and that the individual must find the means to prevent damage. Use of physical exercise, and other distractions produced by pleasant activities, may help to ward off periods of worry and distress. Consulting a trusted friend or a counsellor has considerable advantage in that bringing thoughts and feelings into the open have been found to be beneficial (Pennebaker 1989).

Research by Howarth (1989) has indicated that those who seek help of all kinds may be self-selected by personality factors such as self-esteem. Specifically those with high self-esteem are more likely to benefit from help and advice than those with low self-esteem. Social support has been found to be very important in the lives of most people. Those individuals who have single status for whatever reason may be more vulnerable to stress in work environments; this would be expected from epidemiological evidence to be more true for males than females although the pattern is changing.

Social support may operate by providing distractions from un-happiness caused by stress, or by helping the individual re-work and change personal perspectives on what has happened. The issue is complex and the seeking of social support may be idiosyncratic (for further details see Winnubst 1989).

Summary

Possible methods of coping with major sources of stress in academic staff have been outlined. Overload and administrative load have been identified as major problems for staff. In work stress environments, coping strategies are of two types – those which are problem focused and those which are emotion-focused. Problem focused coping requires a pragmatic approach to the source of difficulty. In the case of academics some action needs to be taken to reduce overload, role switching, and the demands of administrative tasks. Some of the issues raised in the previous chapter are considered. Division of labour within departments creating RATs, TARs, and ARTs, has a number of difficulties and is unlikely to provide a complete solution.

11

Managing Productive Activity in Universities

Reduction of demand and increase in personal control

If people in work environments are to be productive, those in managerial positions should consider the importance of the total demands made and the context in which academic tasks are being carried out. From some of the findings reported in previous chapters, it would seem that academic staff are increasingly both coping with high demand and losing control over many aspects of their traditional tasks. At a time when many companies are emphasizing the importance of personal jurisdiction and discretion, the Jarratt style approach to the management of universities (Jarratt 1985) has had the reverse effects; decision making at the executive level may be too strong for effective intervention by Senate. There is an increased risk of erosion of control when traditional collegiate style of government is replaced by executive groups who are not elected by majority of academic staff. Corporate control loss will translate into loss of research decision making.

Small group-executive style decision making creates distance between the senior offices and the academic 'workforce'. This may have an adverse effect on creativity because pressure can be exerted on staff to carry out extra tasks to cope with increased student numbers without the essential agreement of staff etc. The traditional collegiate style of government if attenuated leaves Senate like a 'rubber stamp' for policies already decided at a higher level. Academic staff may then have little more than a monitoring 'grumbling' or critical role. The importance a university gives to its Senate could well have a very important effect on confidence and productivity of its staff.

It is worth emphasizing that the members of Senate are often in external contexts, major figures in their specialties. Yet prophets in their own land are perhaps not always recognized. Thus major figures with academic skill and experience may not have the necessary influential roles in policy-making.

Managerial aspects of academic practice: Reactions to reform

One of the most important aspects of development in university education concerns the level and quality of research and teaching. In any group or organization there will be those who are creative and successful and those who are less so. In the case of the British university system, nearly all universities were faced with the problem of those with tenure who were not necessarily as productive as was needed to maintain adequate levels of funding. The related problem is to try to change this; but change itself is perceived as threatening by many (see Fisher (1991), chapters 1 and 2). Thus the organizers of change may be vulnerable to pressures to maintain the status quo. Heads of departments and senior professors would be most liable to face those conflicts.

In fact there is now some evidence to suggest that in nearly all organizations those who are not put in the position of implementing reforms are at risk – yet the changing demands of the academic environment and its financial needs, requires that reforming of old practices when needed is carried out. In fact the failure to implement such strategies renders departments at risk. Individuals who have never had grants or never written articles and perhaps who saw themselves as teachers, may have to be persuaded to take up scholarly endeavours leading to publication or to research funding.

Work by O'Day (1974) in the context of corporate management has indicated that reforming policies instigated by individuals often leads to the social and political isolation of the 'reformer' – O'Day identifies the rituals of intimidation that can affect the reformer who articulates the grievances of others and proposes solutions.

Three kinds of threats are argued by O'Day to be practised by groups and by middle management in three distinct ways. The first relates to the threat of innuendo that middle management is in some sense inadequate. The second concerns the sense of moral weakness that the reforming process implies for management. Finally, the middle manager fears higher managerial authority and the implications of any perceived advances for change at lower level in the hierarchy as far as his or her own authority is concerned.

The first 'intimidation ritual' which occurs is what O'Day terms 'nullification'. Immediate superiors will assure the reformer that his assumptions are null and invalid or result from misunderstandings or misperceptions. It is hoped that the power of superiors' assurance will be sufficient.

If this fails, an investigation may be held in which the results will again assure the reformer. Curbing any unfavourable publicity is an important part of nullification. Middle management generally moves to cover up any embarrassing truths in the reformers arguments.

Isolation is a second stage in which middle management seeks to reduce the impact of the reformer's arguments. There may be restrictions of communication links, reduction of allocation of resources etc. On some occasions the reformer may actually be moved to a less visible part of the organization. Unresponsiveness to the reformer's criticism adds to the sense of isolation and is meant to convince the individual of the invalidity of his position.

Direct intimidation measures occur if these other measures fail and include defamation of character. Leeds (1964) is quoted by O'Day as having shown that middle managers resort to less legitimate procedures when all else fails. One aspect of this might be attributing reform to questionable motives, underlying psychopathology or gross incompetence. The reformer is then it would seem, becoming a victim because his or her reputation is being destroyed.

Finally, expulsion which involves the keeping of records, the establishment of independent evidence occurs and cross-examination procedures may be used. The aim is to persuade the individual to leave rather than incur the problems which ensue if an individual is sacked. If the individual decides to stay on then it will be expected that he will lack the motivational strength to 'rock the boat'. O'Day points out that by creating the reformer as a bad person the 'good' organisation can safely close ranks. Corridor gossip and political fixing may also help to put the reformer into the position of low motivation.

Whilst very little research has addressed these issues within the university context it is clear that much of what O'Day has identified could well operate within the system of deans and heads of departments as middle managers. Universities now operate different systems of Departmental governance. The single 'head-master style' head of department who provides the flavour of departmental research, is fast being replaced by groups of professors who can influence policy. The head of department in very productive research departments may often be a senior lecturer, thus freeing the professorate to become research entrepreneurs but incurring the difficulties of power-sharing.

A possible solution to reforming tension and its political impact on groups and departments is to arrange department structures so that there are individuals which function well for the organization because they have self-selected the balance of duties. This would see the end of the need to persuade people who had never obtained PhDs or carried out research and scholarly endeavours to begin doing so.

Co-operative teaching and endeavours depend on good work relationships. The combination of role overload and general overload produced by increased student numbers and higher research demand would be expected to have an adverse effect on social relationships. Some organization of university endeavours is essential for future development.

Self-determined work specialty (SWS) systems

A possible method of reducing the information and task load on academics is to develop particular specialties in principle tasks. This will reduce role overload and will increase the sense of expertise, enhancing personal control and confidence. However, an often mentioned problem is that the separation of research, administration and teaching is thought to have a detrimental effect on teaching.

There is a very good argument for retaining close links between teaching and research because if it is argued that teachers can acquire lectures from books or papers and then present the information constructively to students, this may be just a small step towards appointing 'bare-foot' lecturers, or graduate students who could do the same. Intelligent students are themselves quite competent to do this, and the role of the teacher could be undermined.

The model which may retain the best features which favour productivity is SWS or self-determined work specialty. The individual personally determines a balance of teaching research and administration, but the three elements of research, administration and teaching continue to be part of the role. Thus the links between research and teaching are preserved. In effect RATs, TARs and ARTs are self determined. Individual universities and colleges advertise posts specifying a balance between teaching, research and administration. Advertisements might specify for example, that a research-lead academic in high energy physics was required. Teaching or administration duties could be specified as secondary.

Applicants with the required balance or specialist 'mode' could apply and a promotion structure could be implemented for that particular individual. Thus a teacher-lead professorship would be possible. One of the main benefits might be that the need to produce research would be reduced for those without ideas or inclination. Some individuals could be employed to carry out administration and teaching tasks and would be expected only to spend a small proportion of the week in research and publication. Reduction and narrowing of the scope of research activity would have an overall effect of the 'set aside' academic described in the previous chapter. A more refined and high quality research literature would be an outcome.

Universities could manage the balance per subject in a way that resulted in the best outcome. Some universities could employ a greater proportion of RATs to maintain high academic profiles, others would perhaps like to maximise income from student numbers and could deploy a larger proportion of TARs or ARTs. RATs in these universities might have better access to promoted posts thus ensuring that research continues to be promoted in most universities.

Career changes might occur in-service. Thus a TAR with a sudden set of very good ideas might opt to change balance and the institution might find the possible, if compensatory balances could be achieved. A professor who wished to spend some time developing management skills might shift balance and afford a TAR a stronger research balance.

The focus for research activity: Research institutes

An important issue concerns how research should best be encouraged. For those who are research-led appointments, (RATs) a way of maximizing research effectiveness needs to be found. The concept of a specified group of activities as part of an 'institute' or research centre, would seem to have a number of advantages. Specialized groups of academics and students can bring skills together and can be self-stimulating, developing particular expertise which in turn can be a basis for consultancy.

In industrial settings small structures involving team work have been found to be superior to large assembly line systems, in terms of morale and productivity. On this model, it would be better if research activity could be identified by small autonomous units. An obvious development is to organise those round postgraduate schools. Thus the research director might also co-ordinate teaching of research skills for the postgraduates. This in turn would have the effect of involving and motivating students.

The problem with a small research grouping is that external funding tends to provide one to two year contracts. This means that after a period of training, if further funds for a particular topic are not forthcoming the 'team' is dispersed. Universities may end up training students and staff for employment elsewhere. Although this may be an unexpected benefit for industry and commerce, some action should be taken to reduce its negative effect on research continuity.

One possibility is to allow institutes to make best use of the overheads which are normally part of grants awarded. One way in which this could occur is if the funds could be invested by the institution for the institute so that there is an income which can support continuity of contract posts. If half posts could be created, this would also help to stabilize centres of excellence. Thus a research centre would have an infrastructure which transcended the peaks and troughs of external grant availability and junior academics could in effect be trained to acquire grants as part of a team endeavour.

Summary

Universities are undergoing major change in terms of management practice and job demands. Management practice has moved toward executive style small group decision making which reduces general consultation and control which the collegiate system enhances.

Pressure for research and teaching and the added effect of large student numbers, when employees are already in place, creates the need for change at all levels of the system. Reformers who try to suggest ways in which situations can be improved may be isolated and nullified by the existing system. This is particularly operated at the level of existing middle management who are likely to fear the implications of pressure for change.

The answer may be to have academic staff who are self-selected for particular balances of teaching and research. They then operate within their own perceived specialties. Advertising for different balances of research and teaching may enable departments to cope with change without social strain.

For the focus of research activity, team work in centres of excellence is favoured in that a motivational involvement is likely to be enhanced and a workable infrastructure is developed, based on grant overheads.

References

Albas, D. and Albas, C. (1984) *Student Life and Exams: Stresses and Coping Strategies*. Dubuque, IA: Kendall/Hunt.

Ball, T. S. and Vogler, R. E. (1971) Uncertain pain and the pain of uncertainty, *Perceptual Motor Skills*, 33, 195–1203.

Berkson, J. (1962) Mortality and marital status. Reflections on the derivation of aetiology from statistics, *American Journal of Public Health*, 52, 1318–33.

Bhagat, R. S. (1980) Effects of stressful life events upon individual performance effectiveness and work adjustment process within organizational settings: A research model. James McKeen Cattell Invited Address presented at the American Psychological Association Meeting, Montreal, August.

Bhagat, R. S. (1985) The role of stressful life events in organizational behaviour and human performance. In T. A. Beehr and R. S. Bhagat (eds) *Human Stress and Cognition in Organizations*. New York: John Wiley.

Bills, A. (1931) Blocking: a new principal in mental fatigue, *American Journal of Psychology*, 43, 230–45.

Blumberg, P., Flaherty, J. A. and Morrison, A. E. (1984) Social support networks and psychological adaptation of female and male medical students, *Journal of American Medical Women's Association*, 39, 165–7.

Bowlby, J. (1973) *Attachment and Loss, Vol. 2: Separation, Anxiety and Anger*. New York: Basic Books.

Brady, J. V. (1958) Ulcers in 'executive monkeys', *Scientific American*, 199, 95–100.

Broadbent, D. E. (1958) *Perception and Communication*. Oxford: Pergamon Press.

Broadbent, D. E. (1971) *Decision and Stress*. London: Academic Press.

Broadbent, D. E., Cooper, P. F., Fitzgerald, P. and Parkes, K. R. (1981) The Cognitive Failure Questionnaire (CFQ) and its correlates, *British Journal of Clinical Psychology*, 21, 1–16.

Carranza, E. A. (1972) A study of the impact of life changes on high school teacher performance in the Lansing school district as meassured by the Holmes and Rahe schedule of recent experiences. Doctoral dissertation, Michigan State University.

Conolly, J. (1975) Circumstances, events and illness, *Medicine*, 2(10), 454–8.

Cox, T. (1989) Psychobiological factors in stress and health. In S. Fisher and

J. Reason (eds) *Handbook of Life Stress and Health*. Chichester and New York: John Wiley.

Crown, S. and Crisp, A. H. (1966) A short clinical diagnostic self-rating scale for psychoneurotic patients, *British Journal of Psychiatry*, 112, 917–23.

Dodge, D. L. and Martin, W. T. (1970) *Social Stress and Chronic Illness. Mortality Patterns in Industrial Society*. London: University of Notre Dame Press.

Dolgun, A. (1965) *Alexander Dolgun's Story: An American in the Gulag*. New York: Knopf.

Emmons, C. A. (1982) A longitudinal study of the careers of a cohort of assistant professors in psychology, *American Psychologist*, 37, 1128–38.

Faris, R. E. L. and Dunham, H. W. (1939) *Mental Disorders in Urban Areas*. Chicago: University of Chicago Press.

Fernichel, O. (1945) *The Psychoanalytic Theory of Neurosis*. New York: Norton.

Fisher, S. (1973) A possible artifact in serial response behaviour, *Acta Psychologica*, 37, 243–54.

Fisher, S. (1983) Pessimistic noise effects: the perception of reaction times in noise, *Canadian Journal of Psychology*, 37(2), 258–71.

Fisher, S. (1984) *Stress and the Perception of Control*. London: Lawrence Erlbaum.

Fisher, S. (1985) Control and blue collar work. In C. L. Cooper and M. J. Smith (eds) *Methodological Factors in Occupational Stress*. London: Taylor & Francis.

Fisher, S. (1986) *Stress and Strategy*. London: Lawrence Erlbaum.

Fisher, S. (1988) Life stress, control strategies and the risk of disease: a psychobiological model. In S. Fisher and J. Reason (eds) *Handbook of Life Stress, Cognition and Health*. Chichester and New York: John Wiley.

Fisher, S. (1989) *Homesickness, Cognition and Health*. London: Lawrence Erlbaum.

Fisher, S. (1990) *On the Move: The Psychological Effects of Change and Transition*. Chichester and New York: John Wiley.

Fisher, S. and Hood, B. (1987) The stress of the transition to university: a longitudinal study of vulnerability to psychological disturbance and homesickness, *British Journal of Psychology*, 78, 425–41.

Fisher, S. and Hood, B. (1988) Vulnerability factors in the transition to university: self-reported mobility history and sex differences as factors in psychological disturbances, *British Journal of Psychology*, 79, 1–13.

Fisher, S. and Cooper, C. (1991) *On the Move: The Psychology of Change and Transition*. Chichester: John Wiley.

Fisher, S. and Elder, L. (1992) Psychological aspects of duodenal ulcer or oesophagitis during long term maintenance treatment: the relative merits of a treated ulcer. In J. A. M. Winnubst and S. Maes (eds) *Lifestyles, Stress and Health*. Leiden: DSWO Press.

Fisher, S. and Pemberton, R. (1993) *Report on Stress in the Scottish Prison Service* (to be published).

Fisher, S. and Reason, J. (eds) (1989) *Handbook of Life Stress, Cognition and Health*. Chichester: John Wiley.

Fisher, S. and Smith, P. (1993) *Stress in Academic Staff* (to be published).

Fisher, S., Elder, L. and Peacock, G. (1991) Homesickness in a school in the Australian bush: circumstantial determinants of homesickness incidence, *Children's Environment Quarterly*, 7(3), 15–22.

Fried, M. (1963) Transitional functions of working class communities: implications for forced relocation. In M. B. Kantor (ed.) *Mobility and Mental Health*. Springfield, Illinois: Charles C. Thomas.

Friedman, M., Rosenman, R. and Carroll, V. (1958) Changes in the serum cholesterol and blood clotting time in men subjected to cyclic variation of occupational stress, *Circulation*, 17, 825–61.

Gilbert, P. (1988) The psychobiology of depression. In S. Fisher and J. Reason (eds) *The Handbook of Life Stress, Cognition and Health*. Chichester and New York: John Wiley.

Glass, D. C. and Singer, J. E. (1972) *Urban Stress: Experiments on Noise and Social Stressors*. New York: Academic Press.

Haggard, E. A. (1943) Experimental studies in affective processes: I. Some effects of cognitive structure and active participation on certain autonomic reactions during and following experimentally induced stress, *Journal of Experimental Psychology*, 33, 257–84.

Hamilton, M. (1955) *Psychosomatics*. New York: John Wiley.

Harder, J. J. (1678) Dissertation medico de nostalgi order heimweh praeside. Basle: Johanes Heferno.

Hardy, G. H. (1967) *A Mathematician's Apology*, 2nd edn. Cambridge: Cambridge University Press.

Harris, P. W. (1972) The relationship of life change to academic performance among selected college freshmen to varying levels of college readiness. Unpublished PhD dissertation, East Texas State University.

Hendrick, L. (1943) Discussion of the instinct to master, *Psychoanalytic Quarterly*, 12, 561–5.

Heubner, L. A., Royer, J. A. and Moore, J. (1981) The assessment and remediation of dysfunctional stress in medical school, *Journal of Medical Education*, 56, 547–58.

Holmes, T. H. (1956) Multidiscipline studies of tuberculosis. In P. G. Spooner (ed.) *Personality, Stress and Tuberculosis*. New York.

Holmes, T. H. and Rahe, R. H. (1967) The social readjustment rating scale, *Journal of Psychosomatic Research*, 11, 213–18.

Howarth, I. and Dootjes Dussuyer, I. (1988) Helping people cope with the long term effects of stress. In S. Fisher and J. Reason (eds) *Handbook of Life Stress, Cognition and Health*. Chichester: John Wiley.

Johnson, J. H. and Sarason, I. G. (1979) Recent developments in research on life stress. In V. Hamilton and D. Warburton (eds) *Human Stress and Cognition: An Information Processing Approach*. London: John Wiley.

Karasek, R. A. (1979) Job demands, job decision latitude and mental strain: implicated for job design, *Administrative Science Quarterly*, 24, 43–8.

Kogan, M. and Kogan, D. (1983) *The Attack on Higher Education*. Worcester: Billing & Sons Limited.

Leeds, R. (1964) The absorption of protest: A working paper. In W. W. Cooper, H. J. Leavitt and M. W. Shelly, II (eds) *New Perspectives in Organization Research*. New York: Wiley.

Leff, M. J., Roatch, J. F. and Bunney, W. E. (1970) Environmental factors preceding the onset of severe depressions, *British Journal of Psychiatry*, 33, 293–311.

Lehman, H. C. (1953) *Age and Achievement*. Princeton: Princeton University Press.

Linn, B. S. and Zeppa, R. (1984) Stress in junior medical students: relationship to personality and performance, *Journal of Medical Educational*, 59, 7–12.

Mandler, G. (1975) *Mind and Emotion*. New York: John Wiley.

Mandler, G. and Watson, D. L. (1966) Anxiety and the interruption. In C. D. Spielberger (ed.) *Anxiety and Behavior*. New York: Academic Press.

McDougall, J. B. (1949) *Tuberculosis – A Global Study in Psychopathology*. Baltimore: Williams & Wilkins.

McGrath, J. (1974) *Social and Psychological Factors in Stress*. New York: Holt, Rinehart & Winston.

Mechanic, D. (1959) Illness and social disability: some problems in analysis, *Pacific Sociological Review*, 2, 37–41.

Mechanic, D. (1962) *Students under Stress*. Glencoe: Free Press.

Medalie, J. H. and Kahn, H. A. (1973) Myocardial infaction over a five-year period, I. Prevalence, incidence and mortality experience, *Journal of Chronic Diseases*, 26, 63–84.

Millar, K. (1979) Word recognition in loud noise, *Acta Psychologica*, 43, 225–37.

Miller, G., Gallanter, E. and Pribram, K. (1960) *Plans and the Structure of Behavior*. New York: Holt, Rinehart & Winston.

Moorman, L. J. (1950) Tuberculosis on the Navajo reservation, *American Review of Tuberculosis*, 61, 586.

Oatley, K. (1988) Life events, social cognition and depression. In S. Fisher and J. Reason (eds) *Handbook of Life Stress, Cognition and Health*. Chichester: John Wiley.

O'Day, R. (1974) Intimidation rituals: Reactions to reform, *Journal of Applied Behavioural Science*, 10, 373–85.

Over, R. (1982) Does research productivity decline with age? *Higher Education*, 11, 511–20.

Over, R. (1988) Does scholarly impact decline with age? *Scientometrics*, 13, 215–24.

Over, R. and Lancaster, S. (1984) The early career patterns of men and women in Australian universities, *Australian Journal of Education*, 28, 309–18.

Pennebaker, J. (1989) Confiding traumatic experiences and health, *The Handbook of Life Stress Cognition and Health*. Chichester: John Wiley.

Pervin, L. A. (1963) The need to predict and control under conditions of threat, *Journal of Personality*, 31, 570–87.

Rabbitt, P. (1966) Errors and error correction in choice-response tasks, *Journal of Experimental Psychology*, 71(2), 264–72.

Rahe, R. (1989) Recent life changes and coronary heart disease. In S. Fisher and J. Reason (eds) *The Handbook of Life Stress, Cognition and Health*. Chichester: John Wiley.

Rahe, R. H. and Lind, E. (1971) Psychological factors and sudden cardiac death: a pilot study, *Journal of Psychosomatic Research*, 15, 19–24.

Sarason, I. G. (1972) Anxiety and self preoccupation, *Stress and Anxiety*. Washington: Hemisphere Publishing Company.

Schonpflug, W. (1989) Coping efficiency and situational demands. In G. R. J.

Hockey (ed.) *Stress and Fatigue in Human Performance*. Chichester and New York: John Wiley.

Schuler, R. (1980) Definition and conceptualization of stress in organizations, *Organizational Behaviour and Human Performance*, 25, 184–215.

Seligman, M. E. P. (1971) Phobias and preparedness, *Behaviour and Research Therapy*, 2.

Seligman, M. E. P. (1985) *Helplessness*. San Francisco: Freeman.

Selye, H. (1956) *The Stress of Life*. London: Longmans, Green & Co.

Spiegel, D. A., Smolen, R. C. and Jonas, C. K. (1986) Interpersonal conflicts involving students in clinical medical education, *Journal of Medical Education*, 60, 810–29.

Stewart, A. and Salt, P. (1981) Life stress, life styles, depression and illness in adult women, *Journal of Personality and Social Psychology*, 40(6), 1063–9.

Stokols, D., Schumaker, S. A. and Martinez, J. (1983) Residential mobility and personal well being, *Journal of Environmental Psychology*, 3, 5–19.

Totman, R. (1979) *Social Causes of Illness*. London: Souvenir Press.

Vicino, F. L. and Bass, B. M. (1978) Life space variables and managerial success: their relationship to stress and mental distress, *Journal of Applied Psychology*, 63(1), 81–8.

Weiss, J. M. (1968) Effects of coping responses on stress, *Journal of Comparative and Physiological Psychology*, 65, 251–66.

Weiss, J. M. (1971) Effects of punishing the coping response (conflict), on stress pathology in rats, *Journal of Comparative and Physiological Psychology*, 77, 14–21.

Weiss, R. (1982) Attachment in adult life. In C. M. Parkes and J. Stevenson-Hinde (eds) *The Place of Attachment in Human Behaviour*. London: Tavistock.

White, R. W. (1959) Motivation reconsidered: the concept of competence, *Psychological Review*, 66, 297–333.

Wilkinson, R. T. (1964) Noise incentive and prolonged work: effects of short term memory. Paper presented to the Annual Meeting of the American Psychological Association, Chicago.

Willoughby, L., Calkins, V. and Arnold, L. (1979) Different predictors of examination performance for male and female medical students, *Journal of Amercian Medical Women's Association*, 34, 316–20.

Wolff, H. M. (1953) *Stress and Disease*. Illinois: Charles C. Thomas Springfield.

Yerkes, R. M. and Dodson, J. D. (1908) The relation of strength of stimulus to rapidity of habit formation, *Journal of Comparative Neurological Psychology*, 18, 459–82.

Index

The Society for Research into Higher Education

The Society for Research into Higher Education exists to stimulate and co-ordinate research into all aspects of higher education. It aims to improve the quality of higher education through the encouragement of debate and publication on issues of policy, on the organization and management of higher education institutions, and on the curriculum and teaching methods.

The Society's income is derived from subscriptions, sales of its books and journals, conference fees and grants. It receives no subsidies, and is wholly independent. Its individual members include teachers, researchers, managers and students. Its corporate members are institutions of higher education, research institutes, professional, industrial and governmental bodies. Members are not only from the UK, but from elsewhere in Europe, from America, Canada and Australasia, and it regards its international work as amongst its most important activities.

Under the imprint *SRHE & Open University Press*, the Society is a specialist publisher of research, having some 45 titles in print. The Editorial Board of the Society's Imprint seeks authoritative research or study in the above fields. It offers competitive royalties, a highly recognizable format in both hardback and paperback and the world-wide reputation of the Open University Press.

The Society also publishes *Studies in Higher Education* (three times a year), which is mainly concerned with academic issues, *Higher Education Quarterly* (formerly *Universities Quarterly*), mainly concerned with policy issues, *Research into Higher Education Abstracts* (three times a year), and *SRHE News* (four times a year).

The Society holds a major annual conference in December, jointly with an institution of higher education. In 1991, the topic was 'Research and Higher Education in Europe', with the University of Leicester. In 1992, it was 'Learning to Effect' with the Nottingham Trent University and in 1993, 'Governments and the Higher Education Curriculum' at the University of Sussex in Brighton. Future conferences include in 1994, 'The Student Experience' at the University of York.

The Society's committees, study groups and branches are run by the members. The groups at present include:

Teacher Education Study Group
Continuing Education Group
Staff Development Group
Excellence in Teaching and Learning

Benefits to members

Individual

Individual members receive:

- *SRHE News*, the Society's publications list, conference details and other material included in mailings.
- Greatly reduced rates for *Studies in Higher Education* and *Higher Education Quarterly*.
- A 35% discount on all Open University Press & SRHE publications.
- Free copies of the Precedings – commissioned papers on the theme of the Annual Conference.
- Free copies of *Research into Higher Education Abstracts*.
- Reduced rates for conferences.
- Extensive contacts and scope for facilitating initiatives.
- Reduced reciprocal memberships.

Corporate

Corporate members receive:

- All benefits of individual members, plus
- Free copies of *Studies in Higher Education*.
- Unlimited copies of the Society's publications at reduced rates.
- Special rates for its members, e.g. to the Annual Conference.

Membership details: SRHE, 344–354 Gray's Inn Road, London, WC1X 8BP, UK. Tel: 071 837 7880
Catalogue: SRHE & Open University Press, Celtic Court, 22 Ballmoor, Buckingham MK18 1XW. Tel: (0280) 823388

A HANDBOOK FOR PERSONAL TUTORS

Sue Wheeler and Jan Birtle

This is a sourcebook for personal tutors working in higher education whether in old or new universities or in colleges of higher education. Personal tutoring is a neglected but vital task within universities and the authors highlight the need for time, training and reflective thought.

Most tutors have received little preparation in pastoral care and the emphasis here is on practical guidance. This handbook draws on a wide range of vivid examples through which the complexities of personal tutoring are explored. In particular, it covers the necessary counselling and listening skills, the institutional context, the special problems of adolescent students, of mature and postgraduate students, and of those from culturally different backgrounds.

Sue Wheeler and Jan Birtle are concerned to increase the knowledge base of personal tutors in order to help them become more effective with students while, at the same time, enhancing their own experience and job satisfaction. This book is important reading for all lecturers, essential for all new lecturers, and should be in every university staff induction pack.

Contents
Setting the scene – The role of the personal tutor – Counselling and listening skills – Adolescence – Academic difficulties and study skills – Mature and postgraduate students – Tutoring students from culturally different backgrounds – The personal tutor as part of the pastoral care system – The process of change in higher education – Summary and resources for personal tutors – Appendix – References – Index.

192pp   0 335 09954 8 (Paperback)   0 335 09955 6 (Hardback)

HELPING AND SUPPORTING STUDENTS

John Earwaker

This book offers a critical review of the various kinds of help and support which institutions of higher education provide for their students. John Earwaker begins by looking at students, their problems, their development, and the way they cope with transitions; these are all to be understood in an interpersonal and social context. He then examines the tutorial relationship, drawing out some of the difficulties and ambiguities in the tutor's role. Finally, he offers an explanation for some of the uncertainty in this area, and sets a new agenda for the future. His recurring theme is that helping students is not some kind of 'extra' which may be tacked on as a supplement to the educational experience but is an integral element in the educational process.

Contents

160pp   0 335 15665 7 (Paperback)   0 335 15666 5 (Hardback)

TEACHING AND STRESS

Martin Cole and Stephen Walker (eds)

Teaching is a stressful profession and the radical changes currently occurring in the education system are likely, on balance, to increase rather than reduce levels of stress. There is a danger that media treatment of stress will simplify and sensationalize the matter into one where stress is seen as a pathological state: there is something 'wrong' with the individuals who experience it. Locating the problem of stress in certain individuals is half way to blaming them for their malaise. In fact, *all* teachers experience stress to some degree and this stress is the product of individuals' interaction with their environment. Any discussion of stress must address the teaching environment – the schools, the education system, and their social and political contexts – and the contributors to this volume are well aware of this.

Teaching and Stress explores how we can define, recognize, research and control stress. It examines the nature of stress, its preconditions and its contexts; and proposes a variety of means of managing stress in schools, both at the personal and institutional levels.

Contents
Introduction – Part 1: Understanding stress in teaching – The conditions of stress – Defining stress – Researching stress – Stress and the social context – Containing stress – Part 2: Tackling stress in teaching – Coping strategies – Controlling stress – Stress and training – Stress and educational change – Index.

Contributors
Neil Boot, Susan Capel, Binoy Chakravorty, Martin Cole, Sue Cox, Tom Cox, Jack Dunham, José Esteve, Andrea Freeman, Eric Hall, Chris Kyriacou, Stephen Walker, David Woodhouse, Peter Woods, Arthur Wooster.

192pp   0 335 09547 X (Paperback)   0 335 09548 8 (Hardback)